FOLENS
WORLD
ATLAS

PATRICIA HARRISON   STEVE HARRISON

GU01018740

CONTENTS

ACKNOWLEDGEMENTS

© 2006 Folens Limited, on behalf of the authors.

United Kingdom: Folens Publishers, Apex Business Centre, Boscombe Road, Dunstable, LU5 4RL.
Email: folens@folens.com

Ireland: Folens Publishers, Greenhills Road, Tallaught, Dublin 24.
Email: info@folens.ie

Poland: JUKA, ul. Renesansowa 38, Warsaw 01-905.

Graphics and design: H L Studios
Artwork: H L Studios

The authors and publishers would like to thank the following for permission to reproduce photographs:

Alex Segre Photography p17 (middle right)
Bossu/Sygma p40
Bryan & Cherry Alexander Photography p61
Cleveland County Archaeology Section p10 (top)
Corbis pp9, 12 (bottom), 14 (top), 23 (bottom), 25 (bottom), 32, 39 (top), 41, 43 (top and bottom), 44 (left and bottom), 45, 47 (top), 48 (left and bottom), 49 (left), 50 (bottom), 51, 52 (right), 53 (left), 54, 55 (middle and bottom), 56, 58, 59 (bottom left), 60
Corel p17 (middle)
ESA p34
Fotosearch p50 (middle right)
Getty pp14 (bottom), 17 (top right), 19 (top, middle left and bottom right), 23 (middle right), 33 (top), 48 (right), 52 (left), (55 (top), 57, 59 (top left and bottom right)
Hartlepool Borough Council p10
Inmage p47 (bottom)
Manchester Online p17 (top left)
National Portrait Gallery p30
Nature Picture Library p19 (middle right and bottom left)
Photolibrary pp9, 23 (middle left), 27 (top), 33 (bottom), 39 (bottom), 43 (top), 44 (right), 59 (top right)
Photolibrary Wales p21 (middle right)
Rex Search p17 (middle left)
Still Pictures p49 (right)
Susan Griggs Agency pp12 (top), 49 (right)
SkyScan p14 (middle)
Tony Stone Photo Library p17 (bottom right)
TopFoto p21 (middle left and bottom), p53 (right)

On pages 11, 12, 13, 14, 15, 16, 18, 20 22, 26, 27, 28 and 39 of this atlas, mapping of Ireland is based on the Ordnance Survey with the permission of the Government of the Republic of Ireland and The Controller of HM Stationery Office. Crown Copyright Reserved.

To the best of the publishers' knowledge, information in this atlas was correct at the time of going to press. No responsibility can be accepted for any errors.

First published in 1992 by Folens Limited

Every effort has been made to trace the copyright holders of material used in this publication. If any copyright holder has been overlooked, we would be pleased to make any necessary arrangements.

British Library Cataloguing in Publication Data. A catalogue record for this publication is available from the British Library.

ISBN 184303 848 X

Maps have been used since prehistoric times. They help us understand the world around us.

A map is a way of passing information.

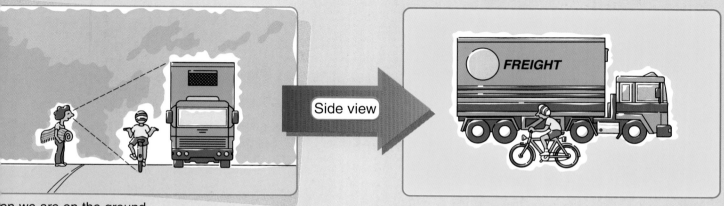

Side view

When we are on the ground we see the world from a side view.

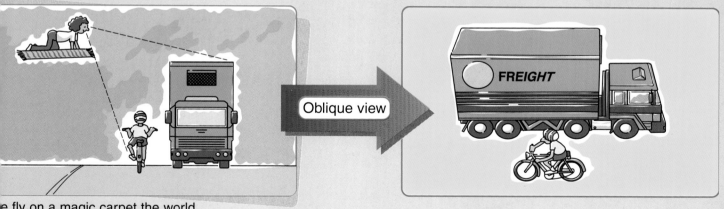

Oblique view

If we fly on a magic carpet the world looks different. This is an oblique view.

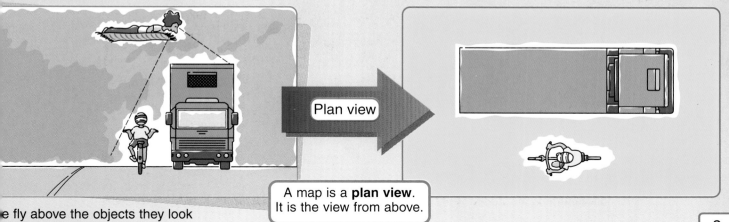

Plan view

A map is a **plan view**. It is the view from above.

If we fly above the objects they look different again. This is a plan view.

Scale

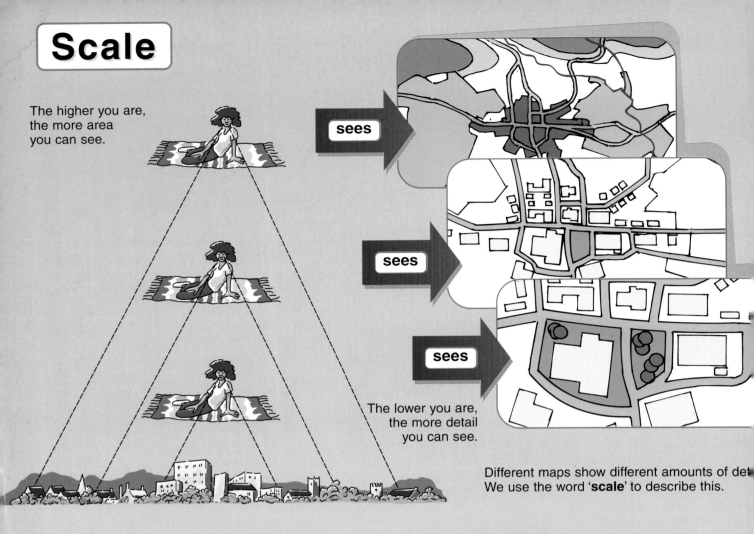

The higher you are, the more area you can see.

sees

sees

sees

The lower you are, the more detail you can see.

Different maps show different amounts of det[ail]
We use the word '**scale**' to describe this.

A builder needs a **large-scale map** which shows the details of roads, pavements and buildings.

A lorry driver needs a much **smaller scale m**[ap] which gives informatio[n] about main roads between towns.

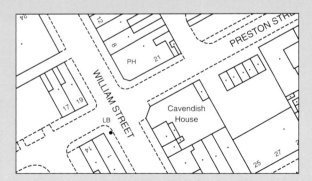

This map would be no use to the lorry driver.

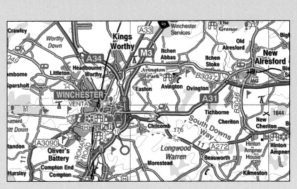

This map would be no use to the builder.

Choosing the right scale of map is important.

Example:
1 cm on the map stands for 1 250 cm on the ground.

0   25 m
Scale 1:1250

Maps show the scale in a scale box.

4

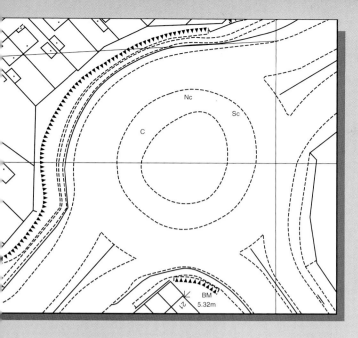

When using a large-scale map we often know what is shown by its shape. Features such as traffic roundabouts, churches, running tracks and docks are easy to recognise from their shape.

Other features are not so easy to recognise. Many buildings have the same shape. In order to show which building is a Post Office and which is a public house, the map maker uses letter symbols.

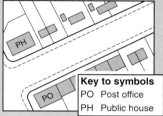

Key to symbols
PO Post office
PH Public house

...me maps have word, letter and picture symbols to help us ...erstand what is shown.

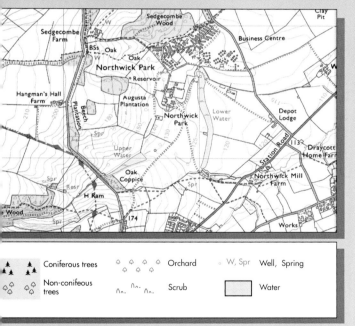

Coniferous trees

Non-conifeous trees

Orchard

Scrub

W, Spr Well, Spring

Water

Map makers also use different colours to make the maps easy to follow.

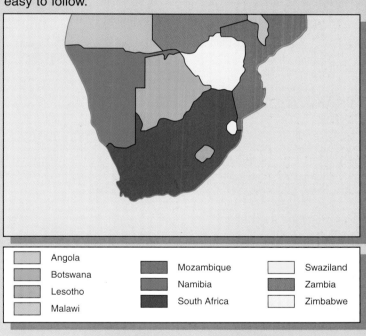

Angola
Botswana
Lesotho
Malawi

Mozambique
Namibia
South Africa

Swaziland
Zambia
Zimbabwe

Map keys

When symbols and colours are used in a map they are usually shown in a key.

The key explains the meaning of the symbols and colours.

The maps in this atlas have their own keys. Read the keys to help you understand the maps.

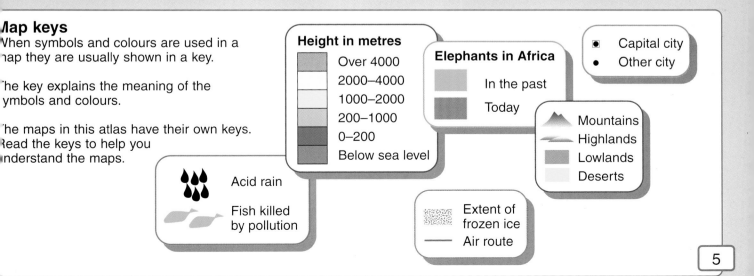

Height in metres
Over 4000
2000–4000
1000–2000
200–1000
0–200
Below sea level

Elephants in Africa
In the past
Today

Capital city
Other city

Mountains
Highlands
Lowlands
Deserts

Acid rain

Fish killed by pollution

Extent of frozen ice
Air route

Using the contents and index

An atlas is a book of maps.

Contents

If you want to find out about a continent or a theme you should first look at the contents page at the front of this atlas.
For example: If you are interested in the mountains and rivers of South America you would look for
South America, Physical
in the contents.

Physical maps tell us about the mountains, rivers and lakes of areas.
Political maps tell us about countries, cities and population.

C

Cairo Egypt **46 D6**
CAMBODIA Asia **42 E3**
CAMEROON Africa **46 C4**
CANADA North America **54 C4**
Canary Islands Atlantic Ocean **47 G6**

name   page number

Cairo Egypt **46 D6**

country   position on page

Index

If you want to find a place such as a river or a city, turn instead to the index at the back of the atlas. Places are listed alphabetically in the index.
For example: If you want to find out about Cairo look under the '**C**' section of the index.

Some places appear on a number of maps in this atlas, e.g. London. They are listed in the index under the page on which they appear at the largest scale.

Grid references

Most pages have a grid around the edge of the map. The horizontal axis is marked in letters A, B, C, etc. The vertical axis is marked in numbers 1, 2, 3, etc. Using grid references helps us locate places quickly. Cairo can easily be found in grid square **D6**.

Use your skills

Turn to the contents.
On which page will you find:
a) The mountains of Asia?
b) The cities of Africa?
c) The countries of South America?
d) The rivers of Europe?

Turn to the World index.
What is the page number and grid reference for:
Dar es Salaam, Berlin, Lima, Washington and Tokyo?
These are the capital cities of which countries?

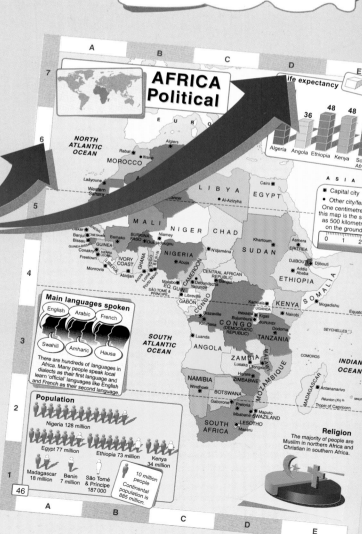

...s can tell us how far one place is from another. To check ...ances we must use the map's scale line.

...ind the distance from Abergavenny to Monmouth, place ...r ruler on the map and measure the distance between the ... town centres.

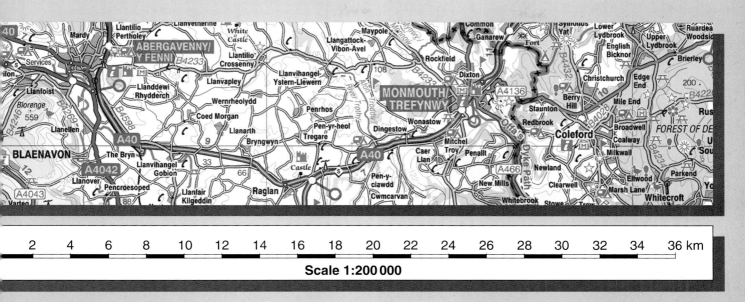

| 2 | 4 | 6 | 8 | 10 | 12 | 14 | 16 | 18 | 20 | 22 | 24 | 26 | 28 | 30 | 32 | 34 | 36 km |

Scale 1:200 000

...easures 10 cm. Check this distance on the scale line. 10 cm is 20 km on the ground. So we know that Abergavenny is ...km from Monmouth.

...ple do not usually travel in straight lines. A better way to measure the distance is to use string. This allows you to follow ...roads as they twist and turn. Using string, measure the distance between Abergavenny and Monmouth (a) on the ...'33 and (b) on the A40. Which route is longer and by how much?

...tinental maps are at a much smaller scale. Use your ruler ...scale line to find the distance between Brasilia and La Paz.

0   1 000   2 000   3 000 km

Scale 1:50 000 000

As well as knowing the distance between places we should also know the direction. By using the eight-point compass we can see that La Paz is west of Brasilia.

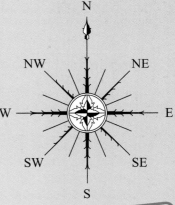

Use your skills

Use the political map of South America on page 50 to find these distances and directions.

Copy and complete the chart. (Distances in km.)

From	To	Distance	Direction
Buenos Aires	Falkland Is.		
Montevideo	Buenos Aires		
Santiago	Brasilia		
Montevideo	Lima		
Caracas	Bogota		
La Paz	Caracas		

Latitude and longitude

The world maps in this atlas have a grid reference system which is used all around the world. The Earth has had imaginary lines drawn on it to help people locate places.

Latitude

Lines drawn horizontally around the Earth are called **lines of latitude.** The first line drawn is where the Earth's circumference is greatest. This line is called the **equator.**

Parallel lines are drawn every 15° north and south of the equator (0°). The North Pole is at 90° north and the South Pole is at 90° south. Lines in-between are described as degrees north and south of the equator.

The lines of latitude are then transferred on to a flat map.

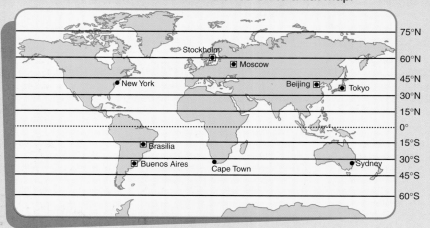

Use your skills

At what line of latitude is (a) Stockholm (b) Brasilia?

Name three cities between latitude 30° south and 45° south.

Between which two lines of latitude is
(a) New York   (b) Tokyo
(c) Moscow   (d) Beijing?

Longitude

Lines drawn vertically around the Earth are called **lines of longitude.** The first line drawn is called the Prime Meridian. It runs through Greenwich, London.

The Prime Meridian was chosen in 1884 because there was a need for all sailors to use the same system and in those days Britain's navy was the largest in the world.

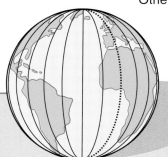

Other lines of longitude are drawn every 15° east and west of the Prime Meridian (0°) until they meet at 180°, close to New Zealand.

The lines of longitude are then transferred on to a flat map.

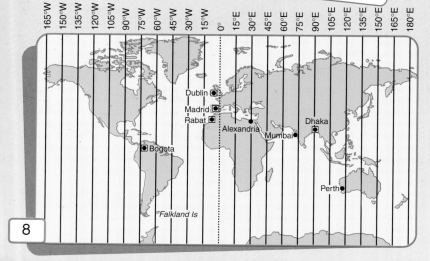

Use your skills

On which line of longitude are
(a) the Falkland Islands
(b) Alexandria (c) Dhaka?

Between which two lines of longitude are Dublin, Madrid and Rabat?

Between which two lines of longitude is (a) Mumbai (b) Perth (c) Bogota?

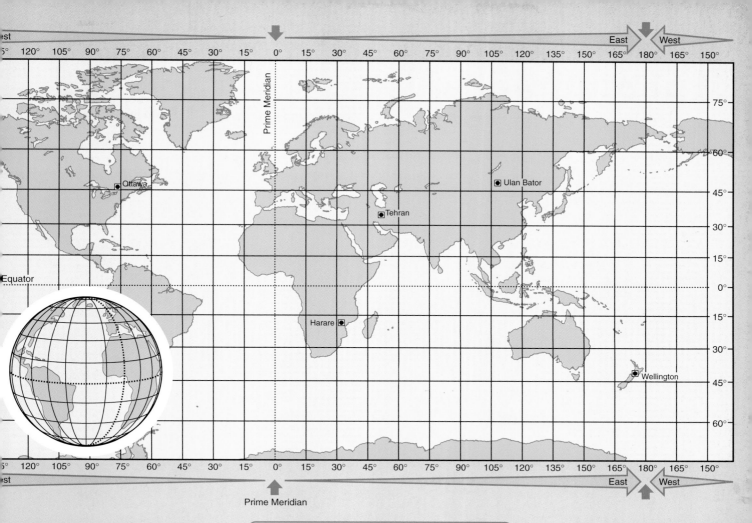

East West

75° 60° 45° 30° 15° 0°

Ottawa
Ulan Bator
Tehran
Harare
Wellington

Equator

East West

Prime Meridian

The lines of latitude and longitude are now combined on a flat map. Any place in the world can be located using two reference points, e.g. Ottawa is at 45° north of the Equator and 75° west of the Prime Meridian. We write this 45°N 75°W.

Use your skills
Which cities are located at
(a) 17°S   31°E
(b) 35°N   51°E
(c) 41°S   174°E
(d) 47°N   106°E?

During the year the Earth tilts as it circles the Sun. In June the Sun's rays are stronger in the northern half (hemisphere) of the Earth. The Tropic of Cancer is an imaginary line marking the point where the Sun is overhead on June 21st.

Tropic of Cancer
Equator
Tropic of Capricorn

Sun's rays June 21st

The Tropic of Capricorn marks the point where the Sun is overhead on December 21st.

Tropic of Cancer
Equator
Tropic of Capricorn

Sun's rays December 21st

There is a strong link between latitude and climate. High latitudes (polar climate) have very low temperatures all year round. Low latitudes (equatorial climate) have hot, wet weather all year round.

9

Aerial photography

Aerial photographs when used with maps provide us with a great deal of information. Look at the photograph for physical features such as rivers or hills and then find them on the map.

Aerial photographs give us information which is not found on maps.

Use your skills
1. What is the highest building?
2. How is the railway supported?
3. What is the weather like?
4. What season is it?
5. What is growing in the fields?

Aerial photograph

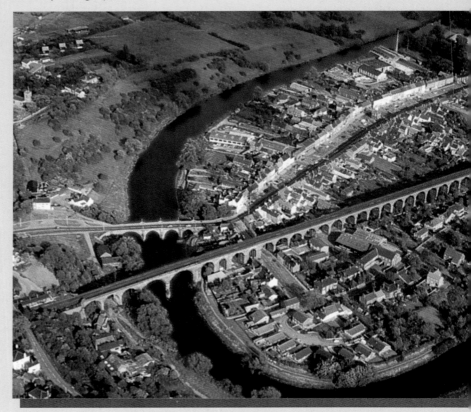

Maps give us information which is not found on aerial photographs.

Use your skills
1. What is this place called?
2. What is the main street called?
3. How many post offices are there?
4. Name the road which passes under the railway bridge.
5. Give the address of the Post Office.

The map has been turned so that it matches the photograph above as closely as possible.

Ordnance Survey map extract

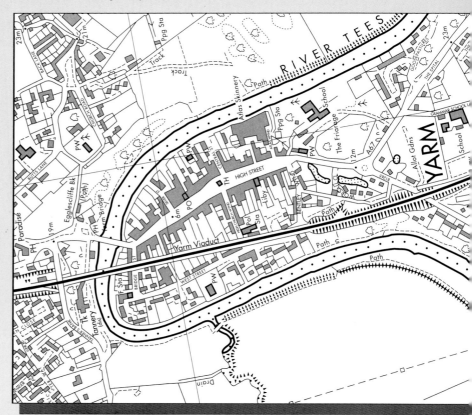

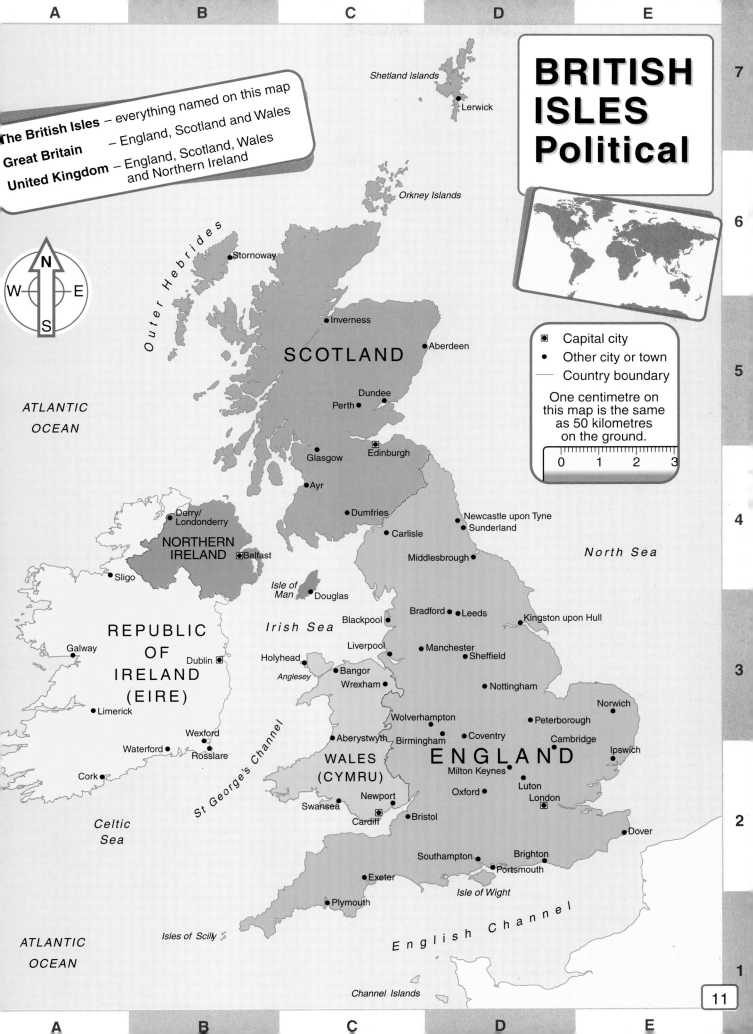

BRITISH ISLES Political

The British Isles – everything named on this map
Great Britain – England, Scotland and Wales
United Kingdom – England, Scotland, Wales and Northern Ireland

- ◉ Capital city
- ● Other city or town
- — Country boundary

One centimetre on this map is the same as 50 kilometres on the ground.

0 1 2 3

A B C D E
7 6 5 4 3 2 1

Shetland Islands
● Lerwick

Orkney Islands

Outer Hebrides
● Stornoway

SCOTLAND
● Inverness
● Aberdeen
Dundee
Perth ●
● Glasgow   ◉ Edinburgh
● Ayr
● Dumfries

ATLANTIC OCEAN

Derry/ Londonderry
NORTHERN IRELAND ◉ Belfast
● Sligo

REPUBLIC OF IRELAND (EIRE)
● Galway
Dublin ◉
● Limerick
Wexford ●
● Waterford   Rosslare ●
● Cork

Isle of Man ● Douglas

Irish Sea

● Carlisle
Newcastle upon Tyne ●
Sunderland ●
● Middlesbrough

North Sea

Blackpool ●
Bradford ● ● Leeds
● Kingston upon Hull
Liverpool ● ● Manchester
● Sheffield

Holyhead ●
Anglesey
● Bangor
Wrexham ●
● Nottingham

St George's Channel

● Norwich

WALES (CYMRU)
● Aberystwyth
Wolverhampton ●
Birmingham ●
● Peterborough
● Coventry
● Cambridge
ENGLAND
● Ipswich
Milton Keynes ●
Newport ●
● Luton
Swansea ●   Oxford ●   London ◉
◉ Cardiff   ● Bristol

Celtic Sea

Southampton ● Brighton ●
Portsmouth ●
● Dover
● Exeter
Isle of Wight
● Plymouth

English Channel

Isles of Scilly

ATLANTIC OCEAN

Channel Islands

N W E S

11

BRITISH ISLES Physical

Height in metres
- Over 1000
- 500–1000
- 200–500
- 100–200
- 0–100

N
W E
S

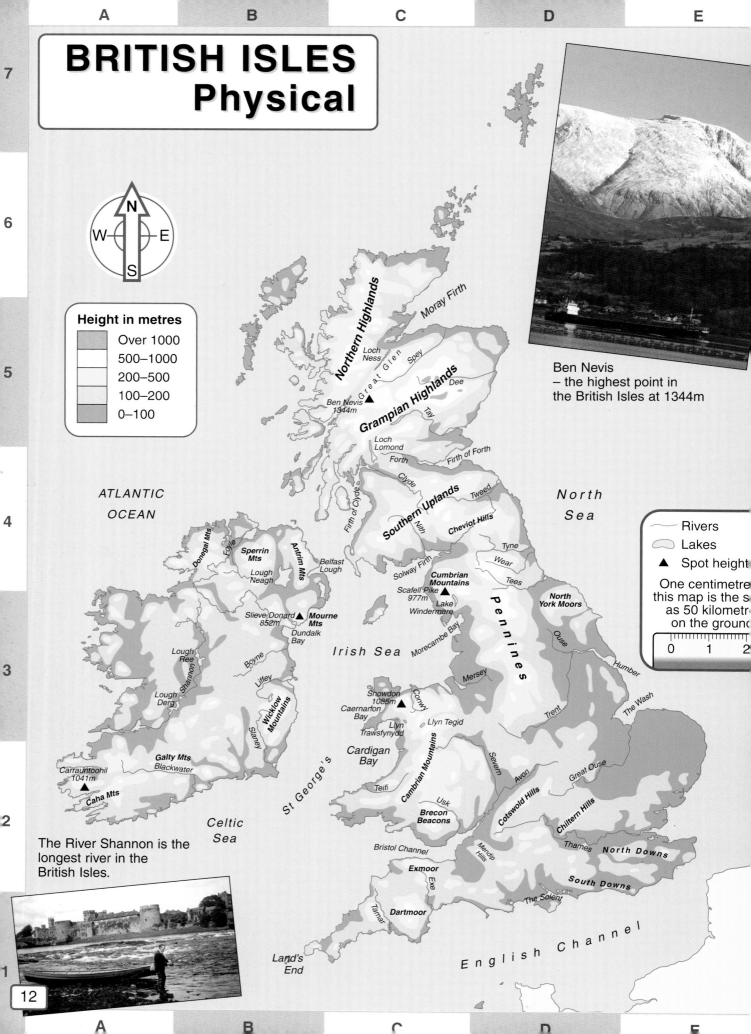

Ben Nevis
– the highest point in
the British Isles at 1344m

Northern Highlands
Moray Firth
Loch Ness
Great Glen
Spey
Grampian Highlands
Dee
Ben Nevis 1344m ▲
Tay
Loch Lomond
Forth
Firth of Forth
Clyde
Firth of Clyde
Southern Uplands
Tweed
Nith
Cheviot Hills

ATLANTIC OCEAN

North Sea

Donegal Mts
Foyle
Sperrin Mts
Antrim Mts
Belfast Lough
Lough Neagh
Tyne
Wear
Solway Firth
Cumbrian Mountains
Scafell Pike ▲ 977m
Tees
North York Moors
Slieve Donard ▲ Mourne 852m Mts
Dundalk Bay
Lake Windermere
Morecambe Bay
Pennines
Lough Ree
Boyne
Liffey
Irish Sea
Mersey
Ouse
Humber
Shannon
Lough Derg
Wicklow Mountains
Snowdon 1085m ▲
Conwy
The Wash
Slaney
Caernarfon Bay
Llyn Tegid
Trent
Llyn Trawsfynydd
Galty Mts
Blackwater
St George's
Cardigan Bay
Cambrian Mountains
Severn
Avon
Great Ouse
Chiltern Hills
Carrauntoohil 1041m ▲
Caha Mts
Teifi
Usk
Cotswold Hills
Celtic Sea
Brecon Beacons
Mendip Hills
Bristol Channel
Thames
North Downs
Exmoor
Exe
South Downs
Dartmoor
The Solent
Tamar
Land's End
English Channel

Rivers
Lakes
▲ Spot height

One centimetre
this map is the s
as 50 kilometre
on the ground

0   1   2

The River Shannon is the
longest river in the
British Isles.

The British Isles are in the path of winds which blow across the Atlantic Ocean. These winds are midway between warm, moist air from the south and cold, dry air from the north. This mixture gives us our very changeable weather.

As the clouds reach the land they start to drop rain. When the clouds rise above high ground they cool and drop even more rain. The west of the British Isles is very wet because the clouds arrive there first. Compare the physical map opposite with the rainfall map. Can you see a connection between high land and heavy rainfall?

Rainfall
(mm)

- More than 1800
- 1200–1800
- 800–1200
- 600–800
- 0–600

rising
air cools;
drops
moisture

rain

rain
shadow

and picks up
moisture
over the sea

January temperatures

In winter, temperatures in the British Isles are lower in the east than in the west, although mountain areas are the coldest of all.

Temperature (°C)

- More than 7
- 6–7
- 5–6
- 4–5
- 3–4
- Less than 3

July temperatures

In summer, temperatures are lower in the north than in the south.

Temperature (°C)

- More than 17
- 16–17
- 15–16
- 14–15
- 13–14
- Less than 13

BRITISH ISLES
Communications

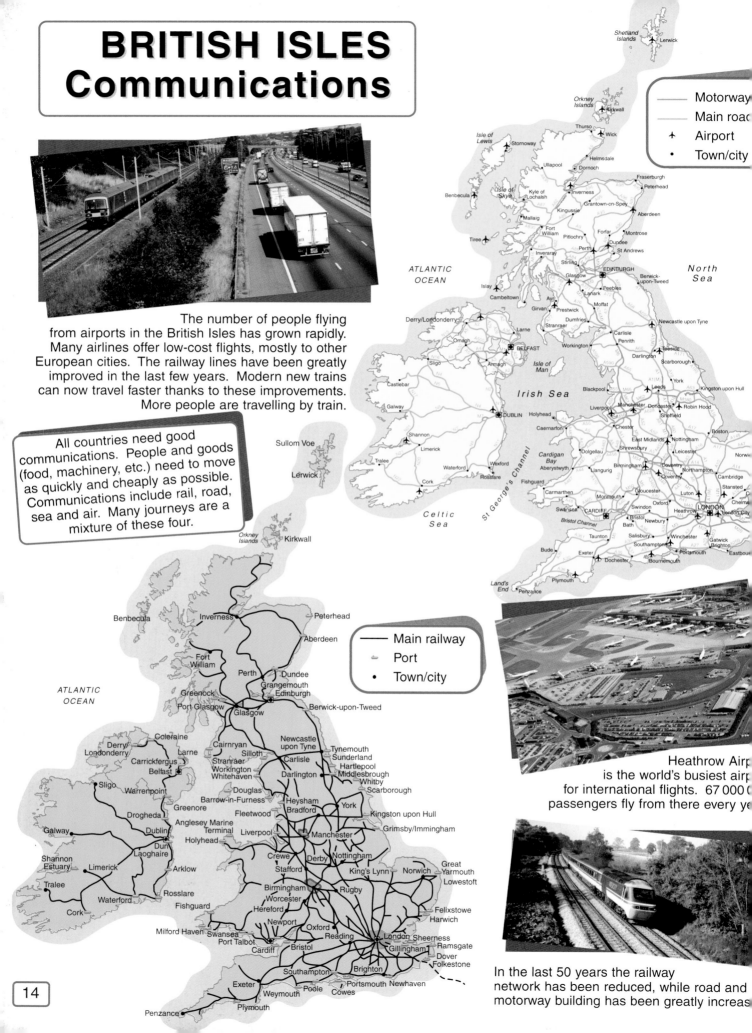

The number of people flying from airports in the British Isles has grown rapidly. Many airlines offer low-cost flights, mostly to other European cities. The railway lines have been greatly improved in the last few years. Modern new trains can now travel faster thanks to these improvements. More people are travelling by train.

All countries need good communications. People and goods (food, machinery, etc.) need to move as quickly and cheaply as possible. Communications include rail, road, sea and air. Many journeys are a mixture of these four.

Legend (top map):
- Motorway
- Main road
- ✈ Airport
- • Town/city

Legend (bottom map):
- —— Main railway
- ⚓ Port
- • Town/city

Heathrow Airport is the world's busiest airport for international flights. 67 000 000 passengers fly from there every year.

In the last 50 years the railway network has been reduced, while road and motorway building has been greatly increased.

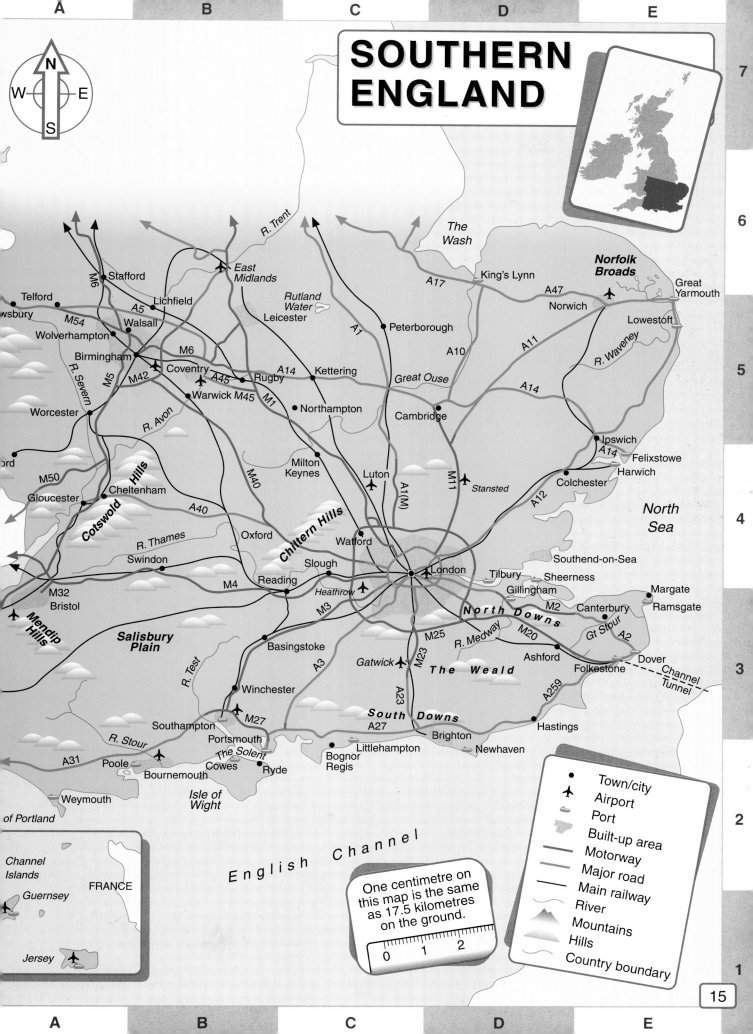

SOUTHERN ENGLAND

N W E S

Map Key:
- Town/city
- Airport
- Port
- Built-up area
- Motorway
- Major road
- Main railway
- River
- Mountains
- Hills
- Country boundary

One centimetre on this map is the same as 17.5 kilometres on the ground.

0 1 2

English Channel

Channel Islands

FRANCE

Guernsey

Jersey

North Sea

The Wash

Norfolk Broads

Places and features:

Telford, Stafford, M6, Lichfield, A5, Walsall, Wolverhampton, M54, Birmingham, M6, Coventry, Warwick, M42, M5, R. Severn, Worcester, R. Avon, East Midlands, Rutland Water, Leicester, A1, A14, Rugby, A45, M45, M1, Northampton, Peterborough, A10, A17, King's Lynn, A47, Norwich, Great Yarmouth, Lowestoft, R. Waveney, A11, Kettering, Great Ouse, A14, Cambridge, Ipswich, A14, Felixstowe, Harwich, Colchester, A12, M11, Stansted, Luton, A1(M), Milton Keynes, M40, Cotswold Hills, Cheltenham, Gloucester, M50, A40, Chiltern Hills, Oxford, R. Thames, Swindon, Watford, Slough, Reading, M4, Heathrow, M3, London, Tilbury, Southend-on-Sea, Sheerness, Gillingham, M2, M25, North Downs, Canterbury, Margate, Ramsgate, Gt Stour, A2, R. Medway, M20, Ashford, Dover, Folkestone, Channel Tunnel, M32, Bristol, Mendip Hills, Salisbury Plain, Basingstoke, A3, Gatwick, M23, The Weald, A259, Hastings, Winchester, R. Test, South Downs, A23, A27, Brighton, Newhaven, Littlehampton, Bognor Regis, Southampton, M27, Portsmouth, The Solent, Cowes, Ryde, Poole, A31, Bournemouth, R. Stour, Weymouth, of Portland, Isle of Wight

R. Trent

15

NORTHERN ENGLAND

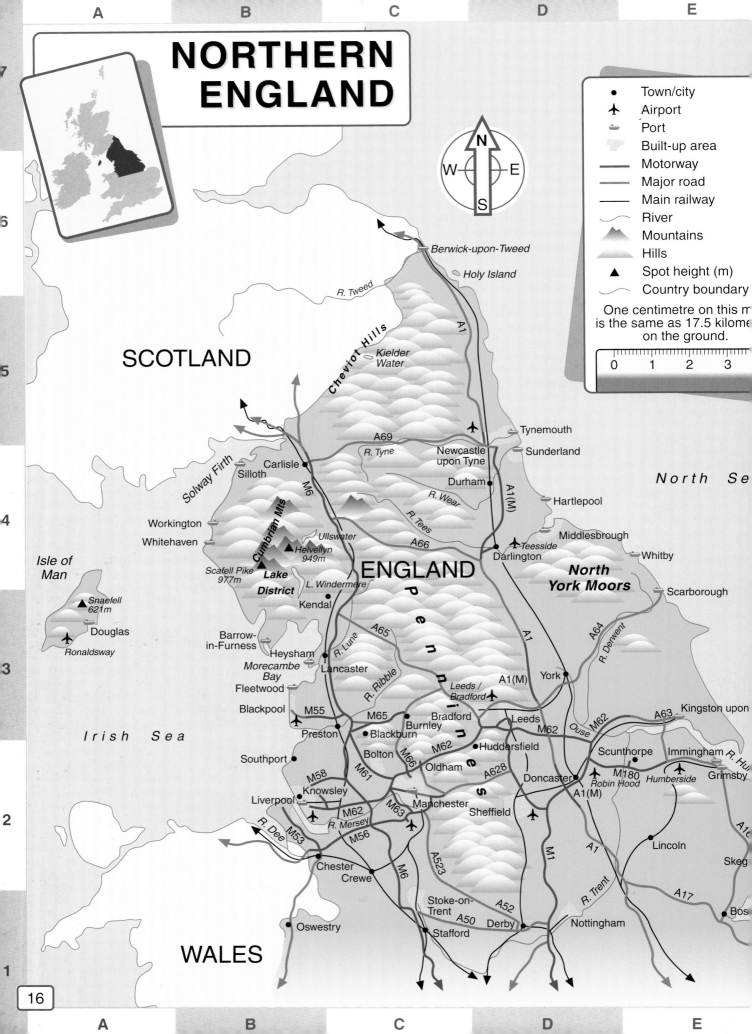

Legend:
- ● Town/city
- ✈ Airport
- ⛴ Port
- Built-up area
- ▬ Motorway
- ▬ Major road
- ▬ Main railway
- ～ River
- ⛰ Mountains
- ⛰ Hills
- ▲ Spot height (m)
- ～ Country boundary

One centimetre on this m is the same as 17.5 kilome on the ground.

0 1 2 3

SCOTLAND

ENGLAND

WALES

Isle of Man

Irish Sea

North Se

Berwick-upon-Tweed
Holy Island
R. Tweed
Cheviot Hills
Kielder Water
A1
A69
R. Tyne
Newcastle upon Tyne
Tynemouth
Sunderland
Carlisle
Silloth
Durham
R. Wear
M6
A1(M)
Hartlepool
Workington
Whitehaven
Cumbrian Mts
Ullswater
Helvellyn 949m
R. Tees
A66
Teesside
Darlington
Middlesbrough
Whitby
Scafell Pike 977m
Lake District
L. Windermere
North York Moors
Scarborough
Kendal
Snaefell 621m
Douglas
Ronaldsway
A65
Pennines
R. Derwent
A64
Barrow-in-Furness
R. Lune
Heysham
Lancaster
Morecambe Bay
R. Ribble
Fleetwood
A1(M)
York
Ouse
M62
A63
Kingston upon
Blackpool
M55
M65
Leeds / Bradford
Bradford
Leeds
M62
Preston
Burnley
Scunthorpe
Immingham R. Hu
Southport
Blackburn
M62
Huddersfield
Doncaster
M180
Grimsby
Bolton
M66
Oldham
A628
Robin Hood
Humberside
M58
M61
Sheffield
A1(M)
Knowsley
M62
Manchester
M1
Liverpool
M63
A1
Lincoln
R. Dee
M53
R. Mersey
M56
Chester
Crewe
M6
A523
A17
Skeg
Oswestry
Stoke-on-Trent
A50
A52
Derby
R. Trent
Nottingham
Bos
Stafford

Solway Firth

16

Traffic congestion in and around large towns has increased year by year. Different solutions are being tried around the country. Bus lanes allow buses to travel faster than cars. This should attract more passengers onto the buses.

In Manchester a new tramway has been laid. Large numbers of people can be taken quickly and cleanly through the city centre. Trams run on electricity and so do not give off exhaust fumes. Attempts to attract more people to use the train depend on clean, comfortable, fast and reliable services.

ge thermal power stations have been built in the coal ng areas of Yorkshire and the East Midlands. The ution that they cause means that their future is under at.

actfile
ngland

Population	49 855 700
Highest mountain	Scafell Pike 977 m
Longest river	Severn 354 km
Largest lake	Windermere 15 km²

Interesting facts:

The River Severn has its source in Wales.

The Norfolk Broads is a habitat for many rare birds and insects. Some, like the Swallowtail Butterfly, live only in the Norfolk Broads. This habitat is in danger. Chemical pollution from farms and an increasing number of tourists threaten this environment.

SCOTLAND

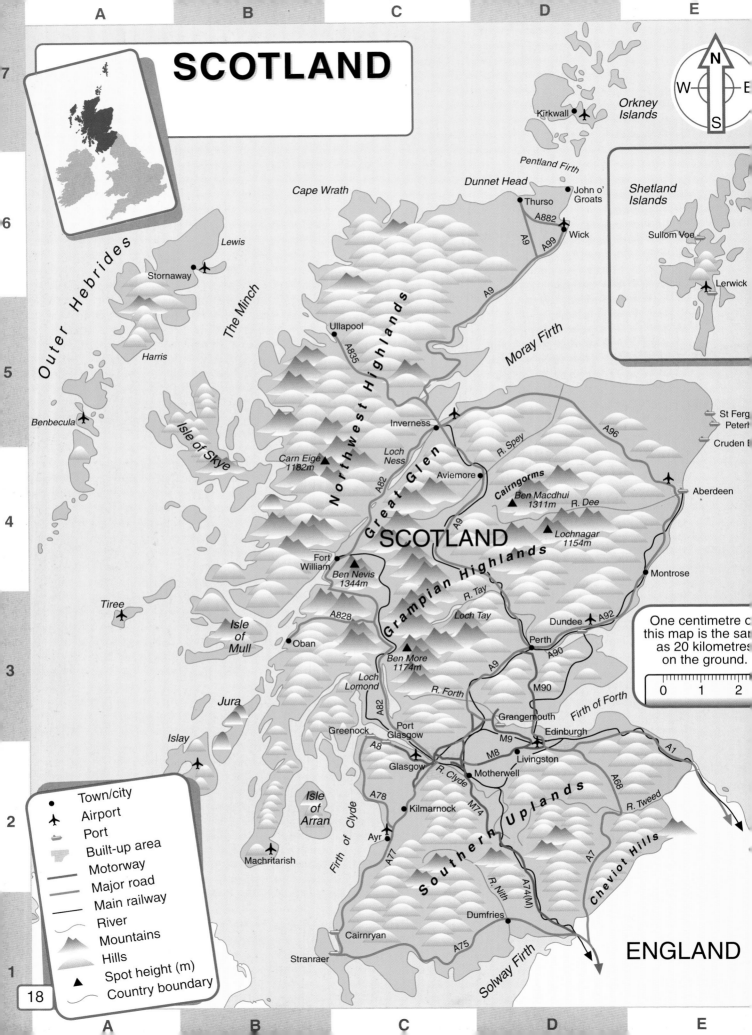

N W E S (compass)

Cape Wrath
Dunnet Head
Pentland Firth
Kirkwall *Orkney Islands*
Thurso · John o' Groats
A882
A9 · A99 · Wick

Shetland Islands
Sullom Voe
Lerwick

Outer Hebrides
Lewis
Stornaway
The Minch
Harris

Ullapool
Northwest Highlands
A835

Benbecula
Isle of Skye

Carn Eige 1182m
Inverness
Loch Ness
A82
Great Glen
Aviemore
R. Spey
A96
Cairngorms
Ben Macdhui 1311m
R. Dee
St Ferg
Peterh
Cruden B
Aberdeen

Tiree
Fort William
Ben Nevis 1344m
A828
A9
Grampian Highlands
Lochnagar 1154m
Montrose

SCOTLAND

Isle of Mull
Oban
Ben More 1174m
R. Tay
Loch Tay
Dundee A92
Moray Firth

Loch Lomond
A82
R. Forth
Perth
A90
M90
Firth of Forth

Jura
Greenock
Port Glasgow
Grangemouth
Edinburgh
A1

Islay
A8
Glasgow
R. Clyde
Motherwell
M9
M8
Livingston
A68

Isle of Arran
A78
Kilmarnock
M74
Southern Uplands
R. Tweed
A7

Ayr
A77
Firth of Clyde
Cheviot Hills

Machritarish
R. Nith
A74(M)

Dumfries
A75
Cairnryan
Stranraer
Solway Firth

ENGLAND

One centimetre d
this map is the san
as 20 kilometres
on the ground.

0   1   2

Legend

- **·** Town/city
- ✈ Airport
- ⛴ Port
- Built-up area
- Motorway
- Major road
- Main railway
- River
- Mountains
- Hills
- ▲ Spot height (m)
- Country boundary

Country boundary

18

...e on the cool, wet, western ...nds has always been hard. ...day, many islands have been ...serted. People have moved to ... mainland to find jobs and a ...re comfortable life. A way of ... that has existed for ...nerations is coming to an end.

Oil and gas were discovered beneath the North Sea in the 1970s. Today, much of the oil is piped to Sullom Voe in the Shetlands and to Cruden Bay near Aberdeen. The main gas lines run to St Fergus north of Aberdeen. Many jobs have been created in the oil and gas industries.

About half of the oil and gas below the North Sea has been extracted. It costs a lot of money to search for, find and then extract the reserves from deep below the sea.

Tourism is an important industry employing many thousands of people throughout Scotland. Glasgow, Scotland's largest city, is now a major tourist attraction. This has helped provide work for people who lost their jobs when older industries were closed.

Tourism needs to be managed. If too many tourists visit the wilder parts of Scotland, they could pose a threat to the wildlife which lives there. Golden eagles and wildcats were once common throughout Britain. It is vitally important that they continue to survive in the Scottish Highlands and that the tourist industry operates in harmony with the natural environment.

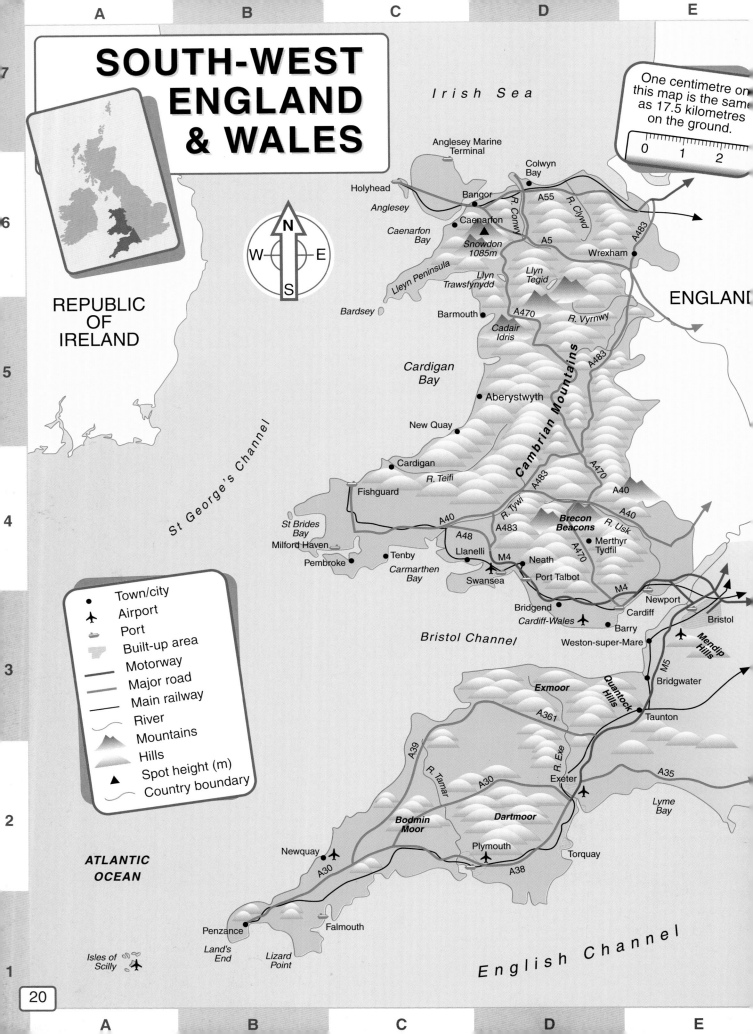

SOUTH-WEST ENGLAND & WALES

Irish Sea

One centimetre on this map is the same as 17.5 kilometres on the ground.

0 1 2

REPUBLIC OF IRELAND

Anglesey Marine Terminal

Colwyn Bay

Holyhead
Bangor
Anglesey
A55
R. Clwyd
A483

Caenarfon
Caenarfon Bay
R. Conwy
A5
Wrexham

Snowdon 1085m

ENGLAND

Llyn Trawsfynydd
Llyn Tegid

Lleyn Peninsula

Bardsey
Barmouth
A470
R. Vyrnwy

Cadair Idris
Cambrian Mountains
A483

Cardigan Bay

St George's Channel

Aberystwyth

New Quay

Cardigan
R. Teifi
A483
A470
A40

Fishguard

R. Tywi
A40

St Brides Bay
Milford Haven
A40
A483
Brecon Beacons
R. Usk

Tenby
A48
Llanelli
M4
Neath
Merthyr Tydfil
A470

Pembroke
Carmarthen Bay
Swansea
Port Talbot
M4

Bridgend
Newport

Bristol Channel
Cardiff-Wales
Cardiff
Barry
Bristol

Weston-super-Mare
Mendip Hills
M5

Exmoor
Quantock Hills
Bridgwater

A361
Taunton

A35

A39
R. Exe
Lyme Bay

R. Tamar
A30
Exeter

Bodmin Moor
Dartmoor

ATLANTIC OCEAN

Newquay
A30
Plymouth
Torquay
A38

Penzance
Falmouth

Land's End
Lizard Point

English Channel

Isles of Scilly

Legend

- Town/city
- ✈ Airport
- Port
- Built-up area
- Motorway
- Major road
- Main railway
- River
- Mountains
- Hills
- ▲ Spot height (m)
- Country boundary

N W E S

A B C D E

Welsh speakers

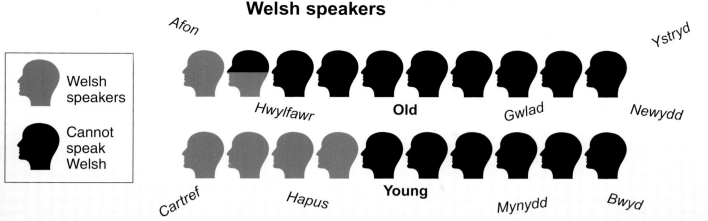

Afon   Hwylfawr   Old   Gwlad   Ystryd   Newydd

Cartref   Hapus   Young   Mynydd   Bwyd

 Welsh speakers

Cannot speak Welsh

For many years Welsh language and culture were in decline. Now attempts are being made to change this. Welsh-speaking schools are increasing and TV programmes in Welsh are more common. Welsh is once again a valued language. According to the last census: Only 15% of adults, aged 20–65, could speak Welsh. However 40% of schoolchildren could speak Welsh.
Welsh is the first language of about 2 out of 10 children born in Wales.

KEEP THE PITS OPEN
Socialist Worker
ALL OUT 2nd APRIL
Socialist Worker
ALL OUT 2nd APRIL
KEEP THE PITS ON

...es was once a major slate- and coal-producing ...ntry. Slate quarrying declined in the 20th century, ...more homes were built using tiles instead of slate. ...e 1980s and 1990s many coal pits were closed. ...usands were thrown out of work. ...rts have been made to attract ...industries to Wales.

...ctfile
...ales

...pulation	2 938 000
...ghest mountain	Snowdon 1 085 m
...ngest river	Usk 105 km
...rgest lake	Llyn Tegid 4.5 km²

...eresting facts:
...n Tegid is the largest *natural* lake.
...rger lakes have been formed by dams.

Tourists from all over the world are attracted to Snowdonia. The castles along the coast are among the finest in Europe. The scenery of the mountains is breathtaking. Wild goats and rare plants can be seen on the higher, wilder slopes. Tourists are encouraged to respect this natural environment so that future generations will also enjoy it.

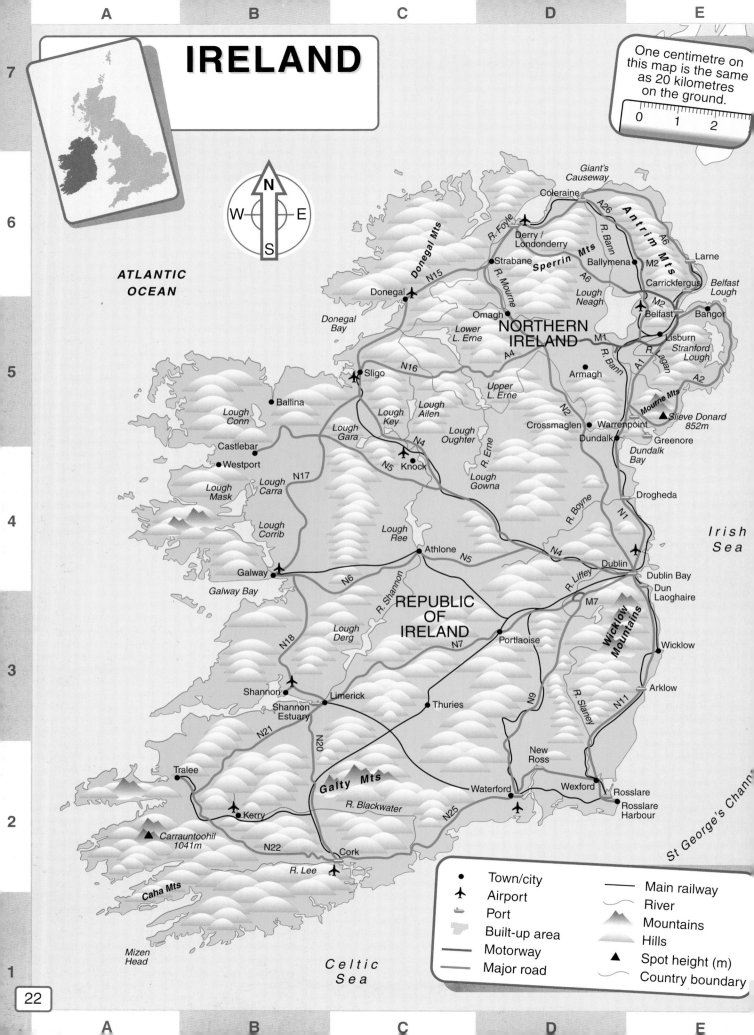

IRELAND

One centimetre on this map is the same as 20 kilometres on the ground.

0   1   2

ATLANTIC OCEAN

N

W   E

S

Giant's Causeway

Coleraine

A26   Antrim Mts   A6

Donegal Mts

R. Foyle

R. Bann

Larne

Derry / Londonderry

Sperrin Mts

Ballymena   M2

Strabane

Carrickfergus

R. Mourne

A6

Belfast Lough

Donegal

N15

Lough Neagh

M2

Belfast   Bangor

Donegal Bay

Omagh

NORTHERN IRELAND

Lisburn

Lower L. Erne

A4

M1

Stranford Lough

R. Lagan

A1

Sligo

N16

Upper L. Erne

Armagh

R. Bann

A2

Ballina

Lough Conn

Lough Gara

Lough Key

Lough Ailen

N2

Mourne Mts

Lough Oughter

Crossmaglen   Warrenpoint   Slieve Donard 852m

Castlebar

N4

Knock

N5

Lough Gowna

Dundalk   Greenore

Westport

Lough Carra   N17

R. Erne   Dundalk Bay

Lough Mask

Drogheda

Lough Ree

R. Boyne   N1

Lough Corrib

Athlone

N5

N4

Irish Sea

Galway   N6

Dublin

R. Shannon

Galway Bay

REPUBLIC OF IRELAND

R. Liffey   Dublin Bay

Dun Laoghaire

Lough Derg

M7

N18

Portlaoise

N7

Wicklow Mountains

Wicklow

Shannon   Limerick

N9   R. Slaney

N11   Arklow

Shannon Estuary   Thuries

N21   N20

Galty Mts

New Ross

Tralee

R. Blackwater

Waterford

Wexford   Rosslare

Kerry   N25

Rosslare Harbour

Carrauntoohil 1041m   N22

Cork

R. Lee

Caha Mts

Mizen Head

Celtic Sea

St George's Chann

Legend

- ● Town/city
- ✈ Airport
- ⚓ Port
- Built-up area
- ━━ Motorway
- ── Major road
- ── Main railway
- River
- 🏔 Mountains
- Hills
- ▲ Spot height (m)
- Country boundary

Emigration from Ireland

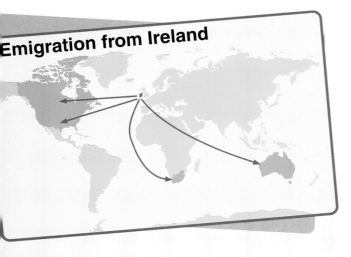

Population of Ireland in the 19th century

Year	Population
1821	(7 000 000)
1841	(8 000 000)
1861	(6 000 000)
1881	(5 000 000)
1901	(4 500 000)

= 1 000 000 people

...h communities are found throughout the English
...aking world. In the USA, for example, they are
...ud to be known as 'Irish Americans'. Over the past
... years, Ireland has seen its people leave to start
... lives in other places.

...ay, Ireland is much more prosperous. Overseas
...npanies have based themselves in Ireland and
...ated many jobs. This has brought a higher
...ndard of living for workers.

The potato blight in 1846 led to 1 000 000 people dying
and 1 000 000 emigrating. By 1870, nearly 2 000 000 Irish
born people lived in the USA and 750 000 lived in
Scotland, England and Wales.

The rivers and loughs of Ireland are
famous. Anglers from all around the world
are among the many tourists who visit
Ireland every year.

...ming is a major industry in Ireland.
... mild climate with its regular rainfall
...eal for the grass crops on which
...ep and cattle feed.

...actfile
...eland

...opulation	5 602 470
...ighest mountain	Carrauntoohil 1 041 m
...ongest river	Shannon 386 km
...argest lake	Lough Neagh 382 km²

...teresting facts:

...bout 3 900 000 people live in the Republic and 1 700 000 live
... Northern Ireland.

After many years of violence between 'Loyalists' who
want Northern Ireland to remain part of the United
Kingdom and 'Republicans' who want British rule to
end, there is now a peace process that encourages
people to work together.

British Isles Index

ANCIENT GREECE

Ancient Greece was not a single country as it is today. It was a large number of small independent states, each located around a city. The largest of these city states was Athens.

Each city state was proudly independent. A citizen of Athens was an Athenian first and a Greek second. People throughout Greece had much in common. They spoke the same language, used the same alphabet, worshipped the same gods and joined together for the Olympic Games.

N

Macedonia

Thrace

Mt Olympus ▲

● Troy

Persian Empire

A e g e a n S e a

Chios

Delphi ●

Corinth ●

X
Salamis

● Athens

● Ephesus

I o n i a n S e a

● Sparta

Kos

Rhodes

	Area of Greek city states
	Persian Empire
→	Route of Persian invasion
X	Battle

Mediterranean Sea

Crete

Early in the 5th century BCE the Persians invaded Greece with a mighty army. The city states of the south came together, fought the Persians and defeated them. Later, the city states fought against each other. The war between Athens and Sparta lasted 27 years.

Greece was united when a northern king, Philip of Macedon and his son Alexander the Great, conquered the south. Alexander went on to establish a Greek empire in North Africa and across Asia to India. Greek ideas and culture were spread far and wide.

INVADERS · AND · SETTLERS

The map shows the routes taken by invaders and settlers from their homelands to Britain. It covers the period from 55 BCE when Julius Caesar landed in Britain, to the year 900 CE when the Viking invasions were almost at an end.

Roman Britain

Although Julius Caesar visited Britain in 55 BCE the Romans did not stay. A full Roman invasion under Emperor Claudius took place in 43 CE.

Invasions
→ Roman
→ Anglo-Saxon *(5th–7th centuries CE)*
→ Viking *(793–900 CE)*

Shetland Is.

700

800

Orkney Is.

North Sea

SCOTLAND

800–840

793

794

867

841

834

IRELAND

Isle of Man

WALES

ENGLAND

855

JUTES

DENMARK

ANGLES

SAXONS

FRISIANS

Caesar (55 BCE)
Claudius (43 CE)

800

840

ATLANTIC OCEAN

Inchtuthil

ANTONINE WALL

Inveresk

Scotland was always a problem for the Romans. They built Hadrian's Wall to keep the northern tribes out of their newly conquered land.
Later they built a second wall, the Antonine Wall, but they never had complete control over Scotland.

Hadrian's Wall was 117 km long and 4.5 m high. It had a large fort every 8 km and a smaller one every 1.5 km.

HADRIAN'S WALL

Carlisle

South Shields

—— Roman road
- - - Roman wall
● Roman town

The Roman Empire

● Rome

☐ Roman Empire

Some Britons welcomed Roman rule. Others did not. The most important rebellion took place in 61 CE when the Iceni tribe, led by Boudicca, fought and almost defeated the Roman army.

York
Brough
Chester
Lincoln
Leicester
FOSSE WAY
WATLING STREET
ERMINE STREET
Wroxeter
Caistor
Gloucester
St Albans
Colchester
Caerleon
Cirencester
London
Richborough
Bath
Silchester
Dover
Chichester
Exeter
Dorchester

Tribes of Ancient Britain 60 CE

VACOMAGI
CALEDONII
TAEXALI
VENICONES
DAMNONI
VOTADIN
SELGOVAE
NOVANTAE
BRIGANTES
PARISI
ORDOVICES
CORITANI
CORNOVII
ICENI
SILURES
CATUVELLAUNI
TRINOVANTES
DOBUNNII
ATREBATES
CANTIACI
DUMNONII
REGNENSES

Roman soldiers from Britain went to fight in continental Europe in 407 CE. Those left behind could not defend Britain from the new invaders. The Roman Emperor told the British that he could no longer protect them. From 409 CE the British were on their own.

Anglo-Saxons

Anglo-Saxon kingdoms

The name 'Anglo-Saxon' is used to describe the peoples who came from the coastal parts of what we now call the Netherlands, North Germany and Denmark.

England was not a single country, it was divided into several kingdoms each ruled over by different Anglo-Saxon kings and queens.

The word 'England' comes from Angle Land – but the invaders were not only Angles. There were also Saxons, Jutes and Frisians.

PICTS

Northumbria

B R I T O N S

Offa's Dyke

Mercia

East Anglia

Essex

Kent

Wessex

Sussex

...n some areas the ...aders replaced or ...arried the native ...tons. In other areas ...small number of ...nglo-Saxons ruled ...er the local British.

...native British were pushed to the ...t of Britain. Only Wales remained ...nquered. From 784 CE to 796 CE ...eat ditch was dug on the orders of ...Offa of Mercia. It marked the border ...een Wales and Mercia. You can ...visit parts of Offa's Dyke today.

The Vikings

Shetland Is

Orkney Is

Viking invaders came to the British Isles from Denmark and Norway. Danish Vikings attacked and settled in eastern and southern England. Norwegians settled in the Scottish islands, the Isle of Man, parts of western Scotland, England and Wales and coastal areas of Ireland.

Main areas of Viking settlement

Vikings ruled over most of northern and eastern England. Their own customs and laws were followed there, so the area was known as the Danelaw.

IRELAND

Isle of Man

Danelaw

WALES

Anglo-Saxons

Wessex

In Ireland, King Brian Boru of Munster led the Irish fightback against the Vikings. In England, King Alfred the Great of Wessex stopped their advance.

EXPLORATION AND ENCOUNTERS
1450–1550

N

Arctic

In the 15th century, most educated people knew that the Earth was round. Explorers believed they could find a short route to Asia by sailing west. What they did not know was that the continents of North and South America were in the way.

John Cabot searched for a northern route to Asia. He reached Newfoundland.

John Cabot (1497)

ENGLAND
• Bristol

Newfoundland

EUROPE

FRANCE

N O R T H
A M E R I C A

NORTH
ATLANTIC
OCEAN

PORTUGAL   SPAIN
Lisbon
• Cadiz

Tropic of Cancer

Christopher Columbus (1492)

San Salvador I

Hernando
Cortez

Area of Aztec
civilization

Christopher Columbus reached the Caribbean Islands in 1492. He crossed the Atlantic three more times and explored the mainland, however he always believed he was in Asia.

A F R I C

NORTH
PACIFIC
OCEAN

Equato

The explorers were soon followed by conquering armies. Hernando Cortez conquered the Aztec Empire (modern Mexico). Francisco Pizarro conquered the Inca Empire (modern Peru). The lives of the people of the Americas were changed forever.

Francisco
Pizarro

S O U T H
A M E R I C A

Ferdinand Magellan (1519)

Area of Inca
civilization

Tropic of Capricorn

Ferdinand Magellan sailed south hoping to find a sea route through South America. Eventually he discovered a 600km passage at the tip of the continent. He sailed through it and reached the Pacific Ocean.

SOUTH
PACIFIC
OCEAN

Explorers' Routes
→ Columbus
→ Cabot
→ Magellan

Conquerors' Routes
→ Cortez
→ Pizarro

Empires of
the Americas

Aztecs

Incas

SOUTH
ATLANTIC
OCEAN

Magellan's
Strait

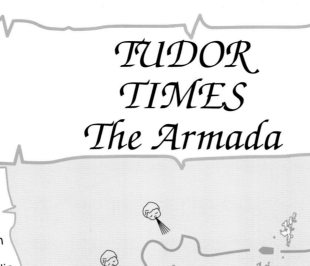

In 6th century Europe, there were many conflicts between Catholics and Protestants. Elizabeth I of England was a Protestant. She became Queen on the death of her half-sister Queen Mary. Mary was a Catholic and married to King Philip II of Spain. Philip was angry with Elizabeth. He believed she was treating Catholics badly in England and that she was helping Protestants in the Netherlands, which was a part of his empire.

(4) Storms drove many Spanish ships on to the shores of Ireland. Survivors were killed as they came ashore because the English feared the Spanish Catholic sailors might join the Irish Catholic people and fight against the English. When the remaining Spanish ships reached home, so many men had died and the fleet was so badly damaged that the invasion of England was no longer possible.

15 Aug 1588

(3) The Spanish decided not to risk another battle in the Channel but to try to reach home by sailing around Scotland and Ireland.

North Sea

SCOTLAND

IRELAND

ENGLAND

London

8 Aug 1588

Gravelines

Calais

SPANISH NETHERLANDS

Spanish Army

19 July 1588

English Channel

ATLANTIC OCEAN

(2) As the Spanish sailed through the Channel they fought the English navy. The Armada had to wait at Calais because the Spanish army was not ready. The English fleet attacked. The next day a great battle took place at Gravelines, Many Spanish ships were damaged.

La Coruña

Santander
*Sept–Oct 1588
70 ships*

Madrid

PORTUGAL

SPAIN

Lisbon
*May 1588
150 ships*

Cadiz

(1) Philip had a large army in the Netherlands. He sent a great fleet of ships (Armada) from Spain. The plan was to meet the army and carry it across the English channel, ready for an attack on London.

Legend:
- Area under English control
- Area under Spanish control
- Route of Spanish Armada
- Spanish ships
- English ships
- Area of fighting
- ★ Battle
- Storm

VICTORIAN BRITAIN

1837

1901

Victoria became Queen in 1837. She died in 1901. Great changes took place in Britain during her reign.

Railways

— Built before 1841
— Built by 1850

In the early part of the 19th century, most goods travelled by canal. This was slow and affected by ice in winter and water shortages in summer. The railways changed all that. The world's first public steam railway ran between Stockton and Darlington in 1825. The first inter-city railway ran between Liverpool and Manchester in 1830. The map shows the great increase in railways up to 1850.

Aberdeen
Montrose
Arbroath
Perth   Dundee
Glasgow   Edinburgh
Berwick
Ayr   Hawick
Newcastle
Carlisle   Durham   Stockton
Darlington   Middlesbrough
Belfast   Scarborough
Lancaster
Leeds   Hull
Preston   York
Liverpool   Manchester   Grimsby
Dublin   Birkenhead   Sheffield
Holyhead   Lincoln
Chester   Crewe   Nottingham
Derby
Stafford   Leicester
Shrewsbury   Peterborough   Yarmouth
Birmingham   Rugby   Norwich
Ely   Cambridge
Gloucester   Colchester
Swansea   Oxford
Cardiff   Whitstable
Bristol   London   Canterbury
Salisbury   Guildford   Dover
Southampton   Gosport   Lewes
Exeter   Dorchester   St Leonards
Plymouth   Portsmouth   Brighton   Newhaven

The population of London rose from 2 685 000 in 1851 to 6 586 000 in 1901. It was the largest city in the world.

City popualtion

1851   1901

The railways and factories needed coal for fuel. Coal production in Victorian Britain increased enormously.

Growth of other UK cities

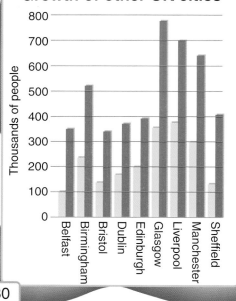

Thousands of people

800
700
600
500
400
300
200
100
0

Belfast
Birmingham
Bristol
Dublin
Edinburgh
Glasgow
Liverpool
Manchester
Sheffield

Railways made trade quicker and cheaper. British cities grew rapidly as people moved there to work in factories and mills. The chart shows the population of Britain's main cities in 1851 and 1901.

Coal production

1840
34 200 tons

1901
222 562 tons

30

THE BRITISH EMPIRE

Britain, like other European countries, began to establish an empire in the 16th and 17th centuries. Some parts of the empire rebelled against rule from London. The USA fought and declared its independence in 1776.

The growth of empire continued into the 19th century. In 1901, the British Empire covered one quarter of the world's surface. One in four of the world's population was ruled over by Queen Victoria.

CANADA

UNITED KINGDOM

BERMUDA

BAHAMAS

BRITISH HONDURAS

JAMAICA

Leeward Is
BARBADOS
TRINIDAD

BRITISH GUIANA

GIBRALTA

MALTA

CYPRUS

BALUCHISTAN

UPPER BURMA

INDIA

HONG KONG

EGYPT

NIGERIA

ANGLO EGYPTIAN SUDAN

BURMA

GAMBIA

SIERRA LEONE

GOLD COAST

BUGANDA

BRITISH SOMALILAND

MALAYSIA

BORNEO

NORTH RHODESIA

BRITISH EAST AFRICA

Ascension

SOUTH RHODESIA

NYASALAND

PAPUA NEW GUINEA

FIJI

St Helena

BECHUANALAND

AUSTRALIA

NATAL
TRANSVAAL
ORANGE
FREE STATE

CAPE PROVINCE

NEW ZEALAND

Falkland Is

Georgia

The British Empire at the end of Queen Victoria's reign

Most of the population of countries like Canada, Australia and New Zealand were descended from British settlers. These countries made many of their own decisions.

Some countries, like India, had been part of the Empire for a long time. Most of the soldiers and officials in British India were Indians.

In Africa, much of the Empire was 'new', brought under British control in the second half of Queen Victoria's reign.

ANCIENT EGYPT

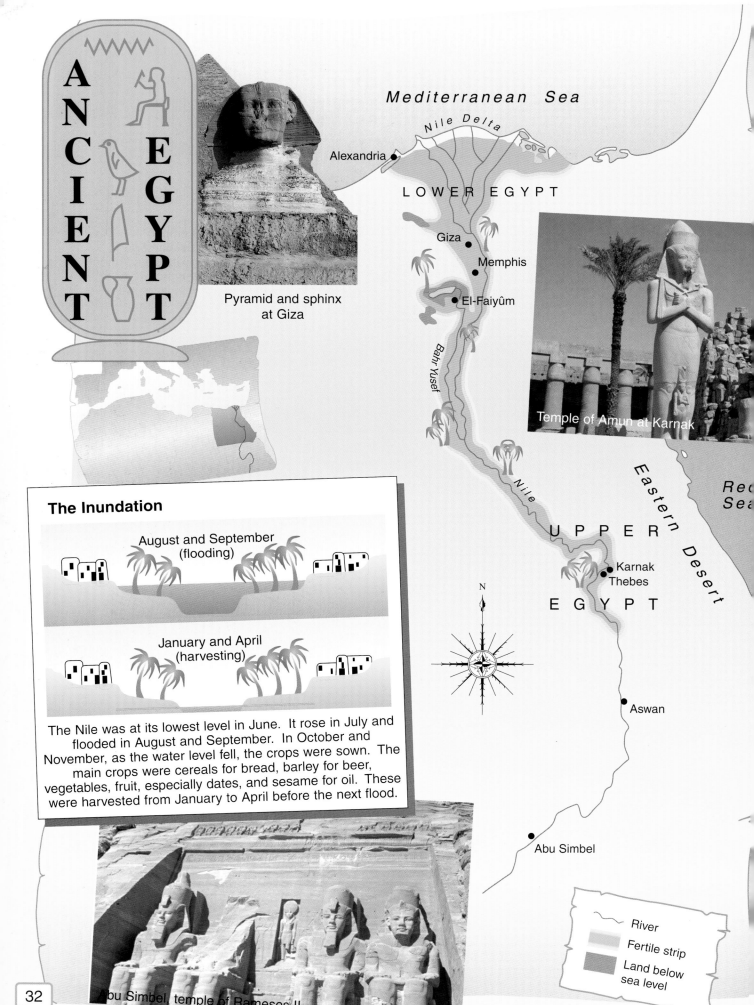

Pyramid and sphinx at Giza

Mediterranean Sea

Nile Delta

Alexandria

LOWER EGYPT

Giza

Memphis

El-Faiyûm

Bahr Yusef

Nile

Temple of Amun at Karnak

Eastern Desert

Red Sea

UPPER EGYPT

Karnak
Thebes

N

Aswan

Abu Simbel

The Inundation

August and September
(flooding)

January and April
(harvesting)

The Nile was at its lowest level in June. It rose in July and flooded in August and September. In October and November, as the water level fell, the crops were sown. The main crops were cereals for bread, barley for beer, vegetables, fruit, especially dates, and sesame for oil. These were harvested from January to April before the next flood.

Abu Simbel, temple of Rameses II

River

Fertile strip

Land below
sea level

The sea covers more than 70% of the Earth. The largest ocean is the Pacific which is four times bigger than Asia. The seas are rich in life but today that life is under threat.

WHOSE OCEAN?

Mediterranean Sea
dly polluted. Most
e pollution comes
the land. Chemicals
in farming, industrial
e and sewage all pour
the sea.

Six million tonnes of oil enter the Earth's oceans every year. Some of this is accidental but much is caused by oil tankers 'washing-out' their tanks.

cies at risk
le numbers have been greatly
ced by hunting. Campaigns from
ervationists have reduced, but not
ped, whaling. Other species such as
dock, herring and mackerel have also
overfished.

e factory ships from Japan and Europe travel great
nces to fish in the seas off West Africa.
se ships can handle up to 1 000 tonnes
h a day. Most of this fish will be
as fertiliser
rms.

l fishing people can
watch as their traditional
n is taken far away.

Fishing with narrow-mesh nets in the Indian and Pacific Oceans has killed many dolphins and porpoises. Today, these nets are made of material which does not rot. Even nets which have broken away from ships continue to trap and kill sea life. When your family buys tins of tuna, check that the tin tells you that care was taken not to catch mammals like dolphins. If not, what can you do?

33

WORLD Political

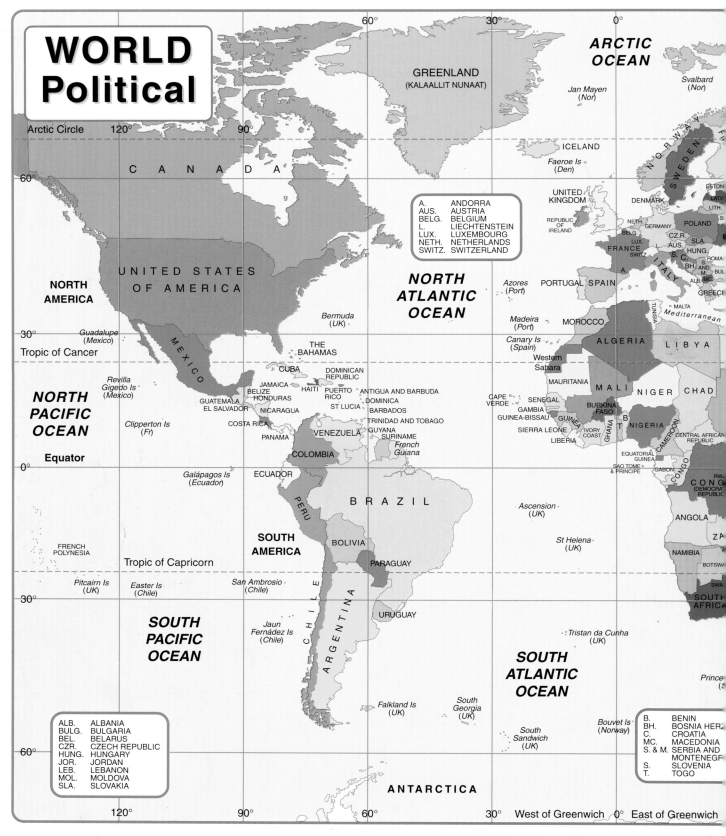

Arctic Circle

ARCTIC OCEAN

GREENLAND
(KALAALLIT NUNAAT)

Jan Mayen
(Nor)

Svalbard
(Nor)

ICELAND

Faeroe Is
(Den)

NORWAY   SWEDEN   FIN

C A N A D A

UNITED
KINGDOM

DENMARK

ESTON
LATV
LITH.
B

REPUBLIC
OF
IRELAND

NETH.   GERMANY   POLAND

BELG.   CZ.R.   SLA.

A.	ANDORRA
AUS.	AUSTRIA
BELG.	BELGIUM
L.	LIECHTENSTEIN
LUX.	LUXEMBOURG
NETH.	NETHERLANDS
SWITZ.	SWITZERLAND

FRANCE   LUX.   AUS.   HUNG.
SWITZ.   S.C.   ROMA
BH.   S.   BUL
AND   MC.
ALB.   GREECE

UNITED STATES
OF AMERICA

NORTH
AMERICA

NORTH
ATLANTIC
OCEAN

Azores
(Port)

PORTUGAL   SPAIN

Bermuda
(UK)

Madeira
(Port)

MOROCCO

TUNISIA   MALTA   Mediterranean

Tropic of Cancer

Guadalupe
(Mexico)

Canary Is
(Spain)

Western
Sahara

ALGERIA   LIBYA

THE
BAHAMAS

CUBA

DOMINICAN
REPUBLIC

HAITI

JAMAICA
BELIZE
HONDURAS

PUERTO
RICO

ANTIGUA AND BARBUDA

DOMINICA

CAPE
VERDE

MAURITANIA

MALI   NIGER   CHAD

Revilla
Gigedo Is
(Mexico)

NORTH
PACIFIC
OCEAN

Clipperton Is
(Fr)

GUATEMALA
EL SALVADOR

NICARAGUA

COSTA RICA

ST LUCIA

BARBADOS

TRINIDAD AND TOBAGO

SENEGAL

GAMBIA

GUINEA-BISSAU

BURKINA
FASO

GUINEA   IVORY
COAST   GHANA   B

NIGERIA

CAMEROON

CENTRAL AFRICAN
REPUBLIC

SIERRA LEONE

LIBERIA

PANAMA

VENEZUELA

GUYANA
SURINAME
French
Guiana

EQUATORIAL
GUINEA

SAO TOME
& PRINCIPE

GABON

CONGO
(DEMOCRA
REPUBLIC

RW

Equator

COLOMBIA

Galápagos Is
(Ecuador)

ECUADOR

Ascension
(UK)

ANGOLA

ZA

PERU

B R A Z I L

FRENCH
POLYNESIA

SOUTH
AMERICA

BOLIVIA

St Helena
(UK)

NAMIBIA

BOTSWA

Tropic of Capricorn

PARAGUAY

SWA

SOUTH
AFRICA

Pitcairn Is
(UK)

Easter Is
(Chile)

San Ambrosio
(Chile)

CHILE

ARGENTINA

URUGUAY

Jaun
Fernádez Is
(Chile)

Tristan da Cunha
(UK)

SOUTH
PACIFIC
OCEAN

SOUTH
ATLANTIC
OCEAN

Prince
(S

ALB.	ALBANIA
BULG.	BULGARIA
BEL.	BELARUS
CZR.	CZECH REPUBLIC
HUNG.	HUNGARY
JOR.	JORDAN
LEB.	LEBANON
MOL.	MOLDOVA
SLA.	SLOVAKIA

Falkland Is
(UK)

South
Georgia
(UK)

South
Sandwich
(UK)

Bouvet Is
(Norway)

B.	BENIN
BH.	BOSNIA HERZ
C.	CROATIA
MC.	MACEDONIA
S. & M.	SERBIA AND MONTENEGR
S.	SLOVENIA
T.	TOGO

A N T A R C T I C A

120°   90°   60°   30°   West of Greenwich   0°   East of Greenwich

60°   30°   0°
120°   90°
60°
30°
0°

The Earth is a sphere. Satellite photographs
give us a clear picture of the Earth in space.
A globe provides a good model of the Earth,
however, it is not easy to carry a globe around
or keep it in a bag! To provide information in
an easy-to-read way, the Earth needs to be
shown on a flat map. The problem with turning a
sphere into a map is that parts of
the sphere need to be stretched
to fit the paper.

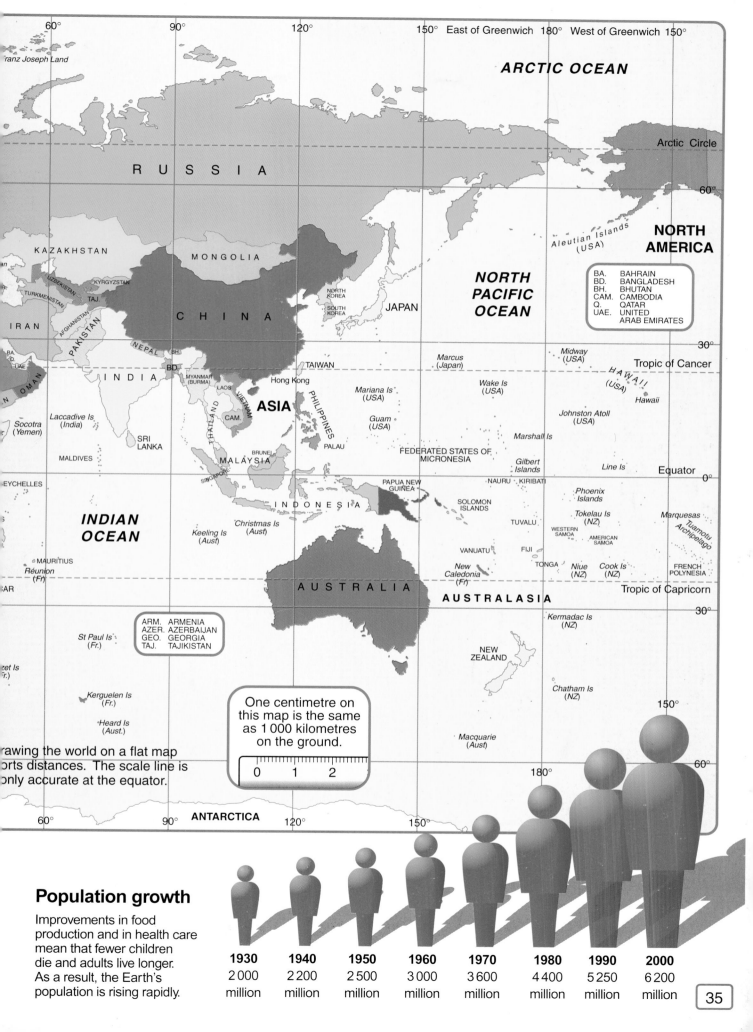

Map labels

ARCTIC OCEAN

Franz Joseph Land

Arctic Circle

RUSSIA

60°

NORTH
AMERICA

Aleutian Islands
(USA)

KAZAKHSTAN

MONGOLIA

NORTH
PACIFIC
OCEAN

BA.	BAHRAIN
BD.	BANGLADESH
BH.	BHUTAN
CAM.	CAMBODIA
Q.	QATAR
UAE.	UNITED ARAB EMIRATES

TURKMENISTAN

UZBEKISTAN

KYRGYZSTAN

TAJ.

NORTH
KOREA

SOUTH
KOREA

JAPAN

AFGHANISTAN

CHINA

IRAN

PAKISTAN

NEPAL

BH.

BD.

Midway
(USA)

30° Tropic of Cancer

BA.
Q.
UAE.

INDIA

MYANMAR
(BURMA)

LAOS

TAIWAN

H A W A I I
(USA)

OMAN

Hong Kong

Marcus
(Japan)

THAILAND

VIETNAM

ASIA

Mariana Is
(USA)

Wake Is
(USA)

Hawaii

Socotra
(Yemen)

Laccadive Is
(India)

SRI
LANKA

CAM.

PHILIPPINES

Guam
(USA)

Johnston Atoll
(USA)

MALDIVES

MALAYSIA

PALAU

Marshall Is

SEYCHELLES

SINGAPORE

BRUNEI

FEDERATED STATES OF
MICRONESIA

Gilbert
Islands

Line Is

Equator 0°

I N D O N E S I A

PAPUA NEW
GUINEA

NAURU KIRIBATI

**INDIAN
OCEAN**

Christmas Is
(Aust)

SOLOMON
ISLANDS

Phoenix
Islands

Keeling Is
(Aust)

TUVALU

Tokelau Is
(NZ)

Marquesas

MAURITIUS

WESTERN
SAMOA

AMERICAN
SAMOA

Tuamotu
Archipelago

Réunion
(Fr)

VANUATU

FIJI

TONGA

Niue
(NZ)

Cook Is
(NZ)

FRENCH
POLYNESIA

New
Caledonia
(Fr)

A U S T R A L I A

AUSTRALASIA

Tropic of Capricorn 30°

ARM.	ARMENIA
AZER.	AZERBAIJAN
GEO.	GEORGIA
TAJ.	TAJIKISTAN

Kermadac Is
(NZ)

St Paul Is
(Fr.)

NEW
ZEALAND

150°

Kerguelen Is
(Fr.)

Chatham Is
(NZ)

60°

Heard Is
(Aust.)

One centimetre on
this map is the same
as 1 000 kilometres
on the ground.

0 1 2

Macquarie
(Aust)

180°

drawing the world on a flat map
orts distances. The scale line is
only accurate at the equator.

ANTARCTICA

Population growth

Improvements in food
production and in health care
mean that fewer children
die and adults live longer.
As a result, the Earth's
population is rising rapidly.

1930	1940	1950	1960	1970	1980	1990	2000
2 000 million	2 200 million	2 500 million	3 000 million	3 600 million	4 400 million	5 250 million	6 200 million

WORLD Physical

Mackenzie

120°

Great Bear
Lake

Great Slave
Lake

**NORTH
AMERICA**

Rocky Mountains

L. Winnipeg

Missouri

Colorado

Mississippi

Rio Grande

Gulf of Mexico

90°

Great
Lakes

St Lawrence

60°

Baffin
Bay

Labrador
Sea

30°

Greenland
Sea

ARCTIC OCEAN

Arctic Circle

Norwegian
Sea

L. Vänern

North
Sea

Rhine

EUROPE

Alps

Danube

Baltic Sea

Mediterranean Sea

0°

60°

Tropic of Cancer

**NORTH
PACIFIC
OCEAN**

30°

**NORTH
ATLANTIC
OCEAN**

Caribbean

Niger

L. Chad

Equator

Andes

Amazon

0°

Zaire

L. Vic

Mt

**SOUTH
AMERICA**

L.

Tropic of Capricorn

30°

Mt Aconcagua ▲

Andes

Cape Horn

Scotia Sea

Antarctic
Peninsula

**SOUTH
ATLANTIC
OCEAN**

Cape
of Good Hope

One centimetre o
this map is the san
as 1 000 kilometre
on the ground.

0   1   2

90°

60°

30°

West of Greenwich 0° East of Greenwich

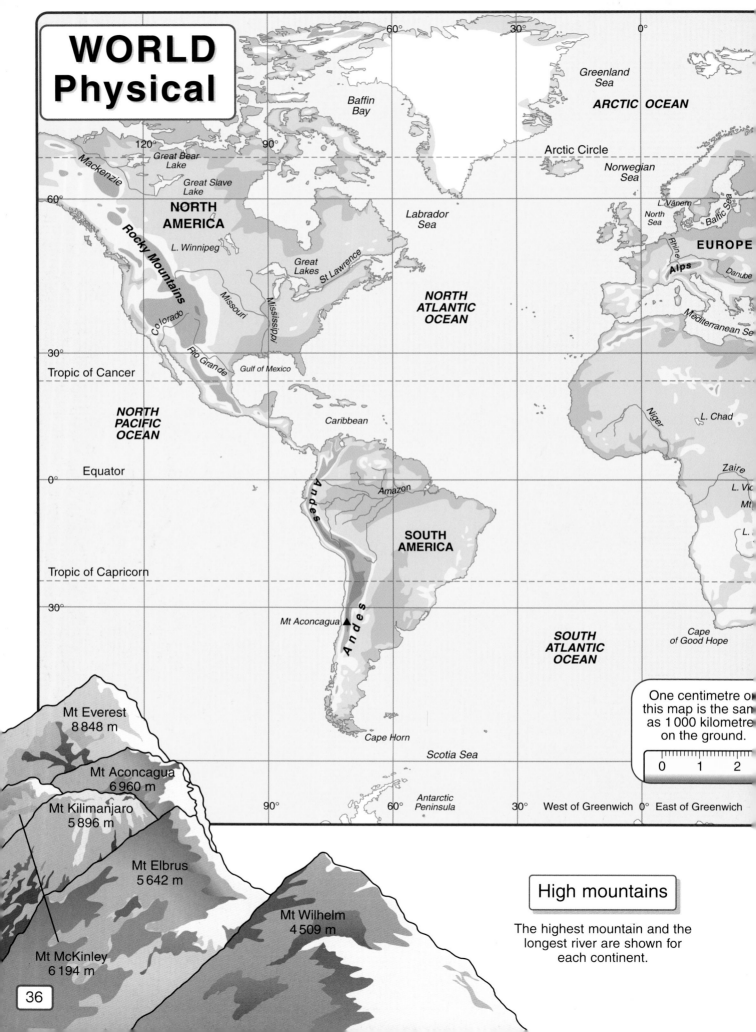

Mt Everest
8 848 m

Mt Aconcagua
6 960 m

Mt Kilimanjaro
5 896 m

Mt Elbrus
5 642 m

Mt Wilhelm
4 509 m

Mt McKinley
6 194 m

High mountains

The highest mountain and the
longest river are shown for
each continent.

36

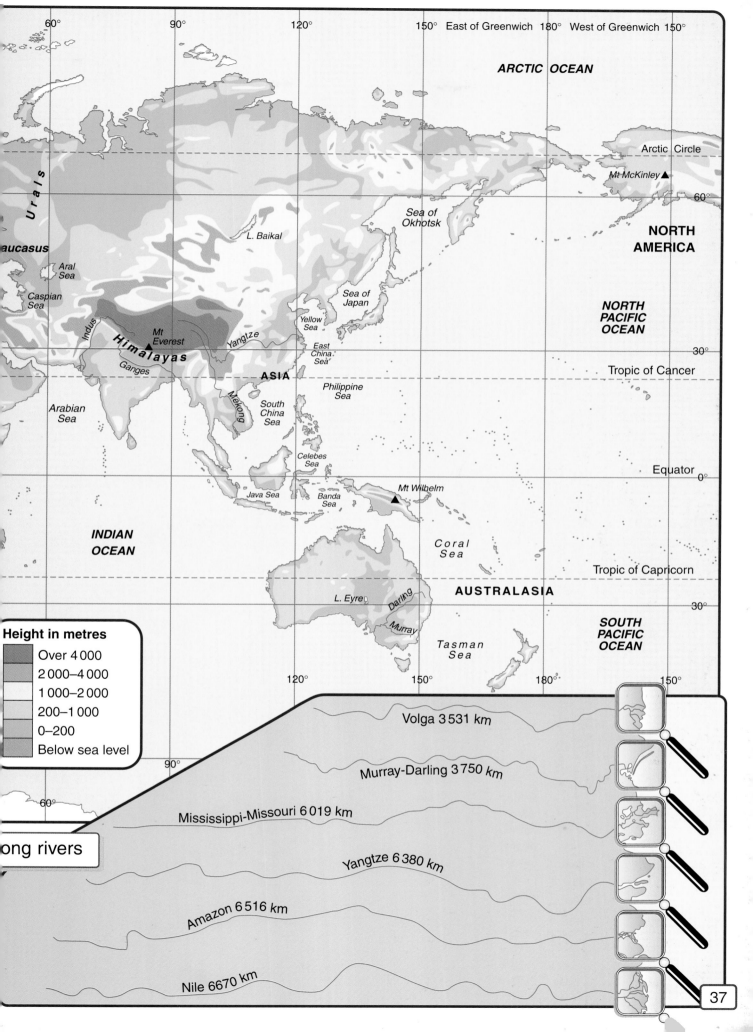

ARCTIC OCEAN

Arctic Circle

Mt McKinley ▲

60°

NORTH
AMERICA

U r a l s

L. Baikal

Sea of
Okhotsk

NORTH
PACIFIC
OCEAN

aucasus

*Aral
Sea*

*Caspian
Sea*

Sea of
Japan

Yellow
Sea

30°

Indus

H i m a l a y a s

Mt
Everest ▲

Yangtze

East
China
Sea

Ganges

ASIA

Tropic of Cancer

*Arabian
Sea*

Mekong

Philippine
Sea

South
China
Sea

Celebes
Sea

Equator 0°

Mt Wilhelm
▲

INDIAN
OCEAN

Java Sea

Banda
Sea

Coral
Sea

Tropic of Capricorn

L. Eyre

Darling

AUSTRALASIA

30°

Murray

SOUTH
PACIFIC
OCEAN

Tasman
Sea

Height in metres

	Over 4 000
	2 000–4 000
	1 000–2 000
	200–1 000
	0–200
	Below sea level

90°

60°

ong rivers

Volga 3 531 km

Murray-Darling 3 750 km

Mississippi-Missouri 6 019 km

Yangtze 6 380 km

Amazon 6 516 km

Nile 6 670 km

120° 150° 180° 150°

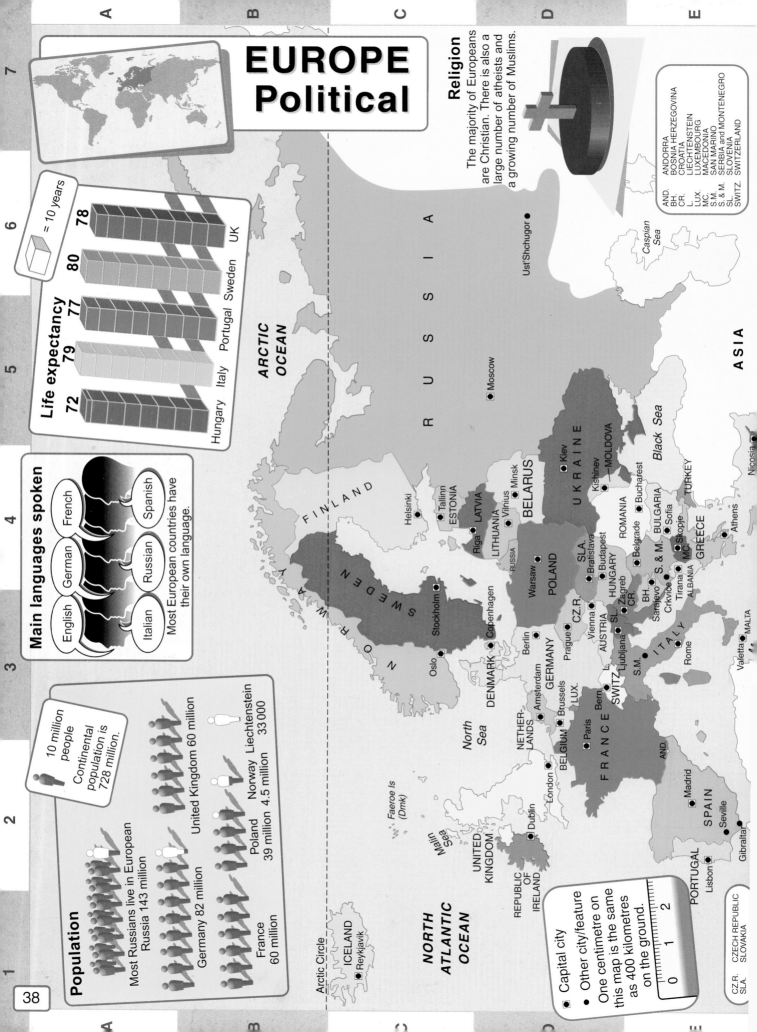

EUROPE Political

Religion

The majority of Europeans are Christian. There is also a large number of atheists and a growing number of Muslims.

AND.	ANDORRA
BH.	BOSNIA HERZEGOVINA
CR.	CROATIA
L.	LIECHTENSTEIN
LUX.	LUXEMBOURG
MC.	MACEDONIA
S.M.	SAN MARINO
S. & M.	SERBIA and MONTENEGRO
SL.	SLOVENIA
SWITZ.	SWITZERLAND

Life expectancy

= 10 years

78 UK
80 Sweden
77 Portugal
77 Italy
79 Italy
72 Hungary

Main languages spoken

English   German   French
Italian   Russian   Spanish

Most European countries have their own language.

Population

10 million people

Continental population is 728 million.

Most Russians live in European Russia 143 million

Germany 82 million

United Kingdom 60 million

France 60 million

Poland 39 million

Norway 4.5 million

Liechtenstein 33 000

Arctic Circle

ICELAND
● Reykjavik

NORTH ATLANTIC OCEAN

REPUBLIC OF IRELAND

● Dublin

UNITED KINGDOM

Faeroe Is (Dmk)

Malin Sea

North Sea

● London

ARCTIC OCEAN

NORWAY

● Oslo

SWEDEN

● Stockholm

FINLAND

● Helsinki

DENMARK
● Copenhagen

NETHER-LANDS
● Amsterdam

BELGIUM
● Brussels

LUX.

GERMANY
● Berlin

● Prague
CZ.R.

● Paris

FRANCE

AND.

● Bern
SWITZ.
L.
S.M.

● Madrid

SPAIN

● Seville

● Gibraltar

PORTUGAL
● Lisbon

● Vienna
AUSTRIA

SLA.
● Bratislava
● Budapest
HUNGARY

SL.
● Ljubljana
CR.
● Zagreb

● Sarajevo
BH.
S. & M.
● Crkvice
MC.
● Tirana
ALBANIA

ITALY
● Rome

● Valetta
MALTA

POLAND
● Warsaw

ESTONIA
● Tallinn

LATVIA
● Riga

LITHUANIA
● Vilnius

RUSSIA

BELARUS
● Minsk

UKRAINE
● Kiev

MOLDOVA
● Kishinev

ROMANIA
● Bucharest

● Belgrade

BULGARIA
● Sofia

● Skopje

GREECE
● Athens

Black Sea

TURKEY

● Nicosia

Caspian Sea

RUSSIA

● Moscow

● Ust'Shchugor

ASIA

● Capital city
● Other city/feature

One centimetre on this map is the same as 400 kilometres on the ground.

0 1 2

CZ.R.   CZECH REPUBLIC
SLA.   SLOVAKIA

38

Hot geyser in Iceland

Ice breaker in the frozen Baltic Sea

EUROPE Physical

Europe's climate ranges from the cold of the Arctic to the warmth of the Mediterranean.

ARCTIC OCEAN

Ural Mountains

Arctic Circle

Norwegian Sea

Lake Ladoga

Volga

Lake Vänern

Baltic Sea

Don

Malin Sea

North Sea

Mt Elbrus

Caspian Sea

Shannon

Thames

Elbe

Rhine

Carpathians

Danube

Caucasus Mts

Loire

Alps

Black Sea

Rhône

Po

Adriatic Sea

Bay of Biscay

Pyrenees

Aegean Sea

NORTH ATLANTIC OCEAN

Tagus

Mediterranean Sea

- ▲ Mountains
- ◿ Highlands
- ▬ Lowlands

Mediterranean beach

Factfile

Coldest place	Ust'Shchugor (Russia) −55°C
Hottest place	Seville (Spain) 50°C
Wettest place	Crkvice (Serbia and Montenegro) 465 cm per year
Highest mountain	Mt Elbrus (Russia) 5 642 m
Longest coastline	Norway 16 093 km
Longest river	Volga (Russia) 3 531 km
Largest lake	Caspian Sea (Russia to Iran) 371 000 km^2

Interesting facts:
The world's shortest border is between Gibraltar and Spain. The Caspian Sea is partly in Europe and partly in Asia. The largest lake entirely within Europe is Lake Ladoga in western Russia close to Finland.

Acid rain

Acid rain is formed when pollution from power stations, factories and vehicles rises into the air and mixes with raindrops. The wind blows the rain clouds. The acid rain often falls far away from the area where the pollution was created. Acid rain affects streams and lakes. Many become so polluted that fish life is completely destroyed. Forests too are being badly damaged by acid rain. In Europe, the polluted air is blown by the SW winds and causes damage in northern Europe and Scandinavia.

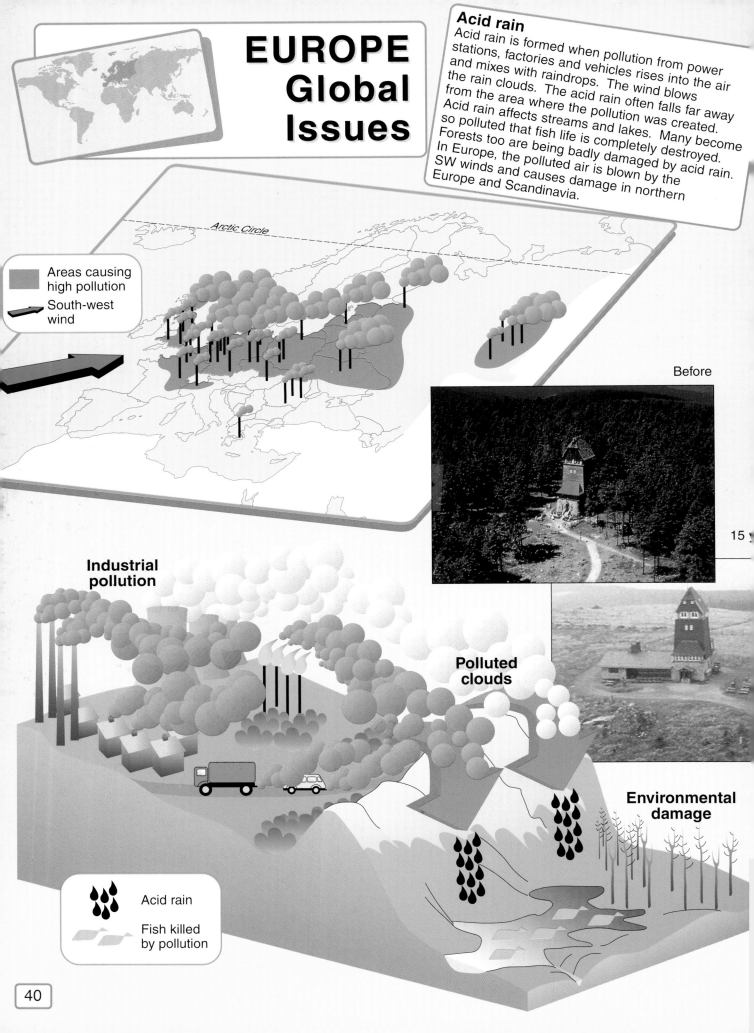

Arctic Circle

Areas causing high pollution

South-west wind

Before

15 y

Industrial pollution

Polluted clouds

Environmental damage

Acid rain

Fish killed by pollution

Gasping for air

Crisis in Athens

During the summer, the air in Athens can be so bad that people die. Athens has grown rapidly in the past 100 years. Millions of people have moved there. On a hot day, fumes from factories and from the large number of old cars stuck in the traffic jams poison the air. If there is no wind to blow the foul air away, it simply gets worse and worse. This not only affects the people. Many of the magnificent ancient buildings of Athens are being damaged by air pollution.

When conditions are really bad, the Mayor of Athens has to take emergency action. Sometimes only cars with four passengers are allowed into the city. There are even days when all cars have been banned from Athens. Other cities around the world have the same problem. In many of them, masks are worn to reduce the effects of the poisonous air.

Parthenon, Athens

GREECE

Athens

Piraeus

As people in the rich world grow richer many families own two or three cars. As standards of living improve in the economically developing world, more and more cars will be bought and driven. What other types of transport will need to be available in large cities if people are to leave their cars at home?

World of cars

The picture shows the number of cars compared with the size of the population. For example, for every 100 people in the USA there are more than 75 cars; in Albania there are fewer than 3 cars for every 100 people.

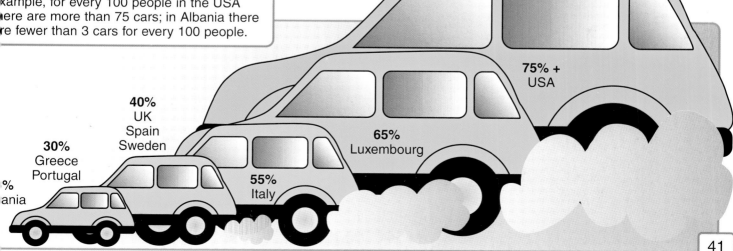

30%
Greece
Portugal

40%
UK
Spain
Sweden

55%
Italy

65%
Luxembourg

75% +
USA

ASIA
Political

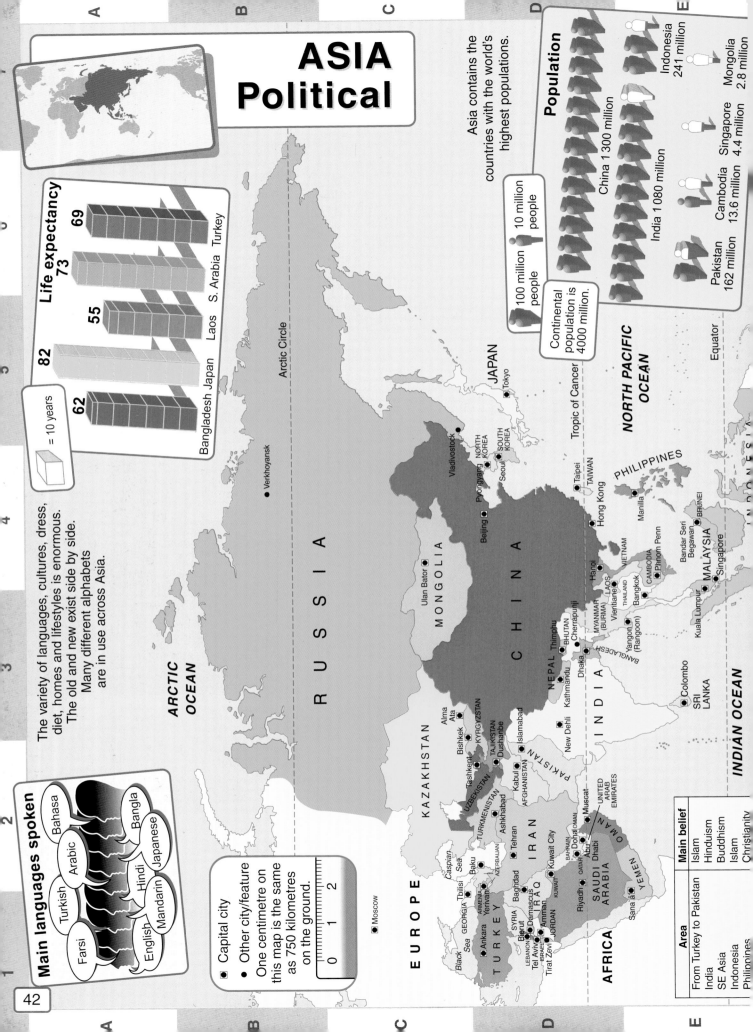

42

Asia contains the countries with the world's highest populations.

Population

100 million people

10 million people

China 1 300 million

India 1 080 million

Indonesia 241 million

Mongolia 2.8 million

Singapore 4.4 million

Pakistan 162 million

Cambodia 13.6 million

Continental population is 4000 million.

Life expectancy

= 10 years

82 — Japan
73 — S. Arabia
69 — Turkey
62 — Bangladesh
55 — Laos

Main languages spoken

Bahasa
Bangla
Japanese
Arabic
Hindi
Turkish
Mandarin
Farsi
English

The variety of languages, cultures, dress, diet, homes and lifestyles is enormous. The old and new exist side by side. Many different alphabets are in use across Asia.

- Capital city
- Other city/feature

One centimetre on this map is the same as 750 kilometres on the ground.

0   1   2

Area	Main belief
From Turkey to Pakistan	Islam
India	Hinduism
SE Asia	Buddhism
Indonesia	Islam
Philipines	Christianity

ARCTIC OCEAN

Arctic Circle

RUSSIA

Verkhoyansk

Moscow

EUROPE

MONGOLIA
Ulan Bator

CHINA
Beijing

NORTH KOREA
Pyongyang
SOUTH KOREA
Seoul

Vladivostock

JAPAN
Tokyo

Taipei
TAIWAN

Hong Kong

PHILIPPINES
Manilla

Tropic of Cancer

NORTH PACIFIC OCEAN

Equator

KAZAKHSTAN
Alma Ata
Bishkek
KYRGYZSTAN
Tashkent
UZBEKISTAN
TAJIKISTAN
Dushanbe
TURKMENISTAN
Ashkhabad
Islamabad
Kabul
AFGHANISTAN
PAKISTAN

NEPAL
Kathmandu
Thimphu
BHUTAN
Cherrapunji
New Dehli
INDIA
Dhaka
BANGLADESH
MYANMAR (BURMA)
LAOS
Vientiane
THAILAND
Bangkok
Yangon (Rangoon)
VIETNAM
Hanoi
CAMBODIA
Phnom Penh
Bandar Seri Begawan
BRUNEI
MALAYSIA
Kuala Lumpur
Singapore
INDONESIA

Colombo
SRI LANKA

INDIAN OCEAN

Tehran
IRAN
Baku
AZERBAIJAN
ARMENIA
Yerevan
GEORGIA
Tbilisi
Black Sea
Caspian Sea
TURKEY
Ankara
SYRIA
Damascus
LEBANON
Beirut
ISRAEL
Tel Aviv
Tirat Zevi
JORDAN
Amman
IRAQ
Baghdad
KUWAIT
Kuwait City
BAHRAIN
QATAR
Doha
Abu Dhabi
UNITED ARAB EMIRATES
OMAN
Muscat
SAUDI ARABIA
Riyadh
YEMEN
Sana'ā

AFRICA

e climates of Asia range from
extreme cold of Arctic Russia
he intense heat of equatorial
onesia.

bian Desert

Taiga

ASIA
Physical

ARCTIC OCEAN

Ural Mts

Siberia

Arctic Circle

Steppes

Aral Sea

Caspian Sea

Lake Baikal

Tien Shan

Altai

Gobi Desert

rabian sert

Persian Gulf

Indus

Himalayas

Mt Everest ▲

Ganges

Brahmaputra

Yangtze

Sea of Japan

Arabian Sea

Bay of Bengal

Mekong

NORTH PACIFIC OCEAN

INDIAN OCEAN

Sumatera

Borneo

South China Sea

Philippine Sea

Tropic of Cancer

Mountains
Highlands
Lowlands
Deserts

Equator

actfile

oldest place	Verkhoyansk (Russia) –68°C
ottest place	Tirat Zevi (Israel) 54°C
ettest place	Cherrapunji (India) 1 143 cm per year
ghest mountain	Mt Everest (Nepal/China) 8 848 m
ongest coastline	Indonesia 54 716 km
ongest river	Yangtze [Chang Jiang] (China) 6 300 km
argest lake	Caspian Sea (Russia to Iran) 371 000 km²

teresting facts:

sia is the world's largest continent; it covers almost one third of the
rld's land space.

xty per cent of the world's population live in Asia. The world's longest
lway is the Trans-Siberian Railway, which is 9 438 km long, and links
oscow with Vladivostok.

Mount Everest

ASIA Global Issues

The growth of the world's population leads to an increased demand on food and other resources. Europe had its rapid population growth in the 19th century. Today growth is greatest in Asia, Central and South America.

The problem

Housing and feeding a growing population is not easy. Different counties try different methods of dealing with this challenge.

China: the response

In China, people are not allowed to move from the countryside to the city without permission. This is to avoid large numbers of homeless people living in shanty towns. Parents in most of China are expected to have only one child.

Indonesia: the response

Indonesia is a country of many islands. Peo from the main islands such as Jawa are giv land in other parts of Indone including Irian Ja

C H I N A

Tropic of Cancer

Equator

I N D O N E S I A

One problem now facing China is that of spoilt children. Grandparents and relatives give so much time and attention to the only child that many now have the nickname 'The Little Emperor'.

The native people of Iri Jaya have seen their forests destroyed to provide land for the nev settlers. Today, many natives, whose families have lived there for generations, are fightin the Indonesian government and demanding independer and an end to the settlements.

Monsoon areas of the world

As summer comes to monsoon areas the land warms up. The air above it rises and fresh air is drawn from over the ocean. This air is heavy with water which has evaporated from the sea. Clouds travel and pass over the land where they drop enormous quantities of rain. In South Asia, the wind carries moisture from the Indian Ocean to the surrounding land.

Many parts of the world around the tropics depend on heavy rain for the crops to grow. This rain is seasonal and is known as the monsoon. The monsoon should mean good news for the farmers but sometimes it means disaster.

Natural disasters

A hurricane develops

Sometimes the monsoon can turn into a hurricane. A hurricane spins as it crosses the ocean. It collects more and more rain as it travels. Hurricane force winds develop. Giant waves are formed. They can destroy everything on low-lying land.

Water evaporates from the ocean.

Sun's rays

Rain clouds form; winds strengthen over the ocean.

Rain clouds and strong winds spiral towards the land. Giant waves form.

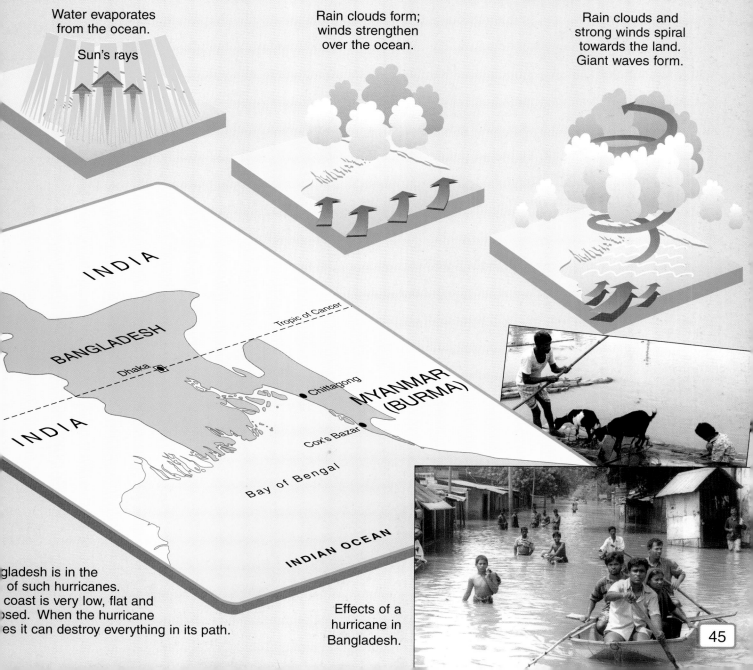

INDIA

BANGLADESH

Dhaka

Tropic of Cancer

INDIA

Chittagong

MYANMAR (BURMA)

Cox's Bazar

Bay of Bengal

INDIAN OCEAN

Bangladesh is in the path of such hurricanes. The coast is very low, flat and exposed. When the hurricane arrives it can destroy everything in its path.

Effects of a hurricane in Bangladesh.

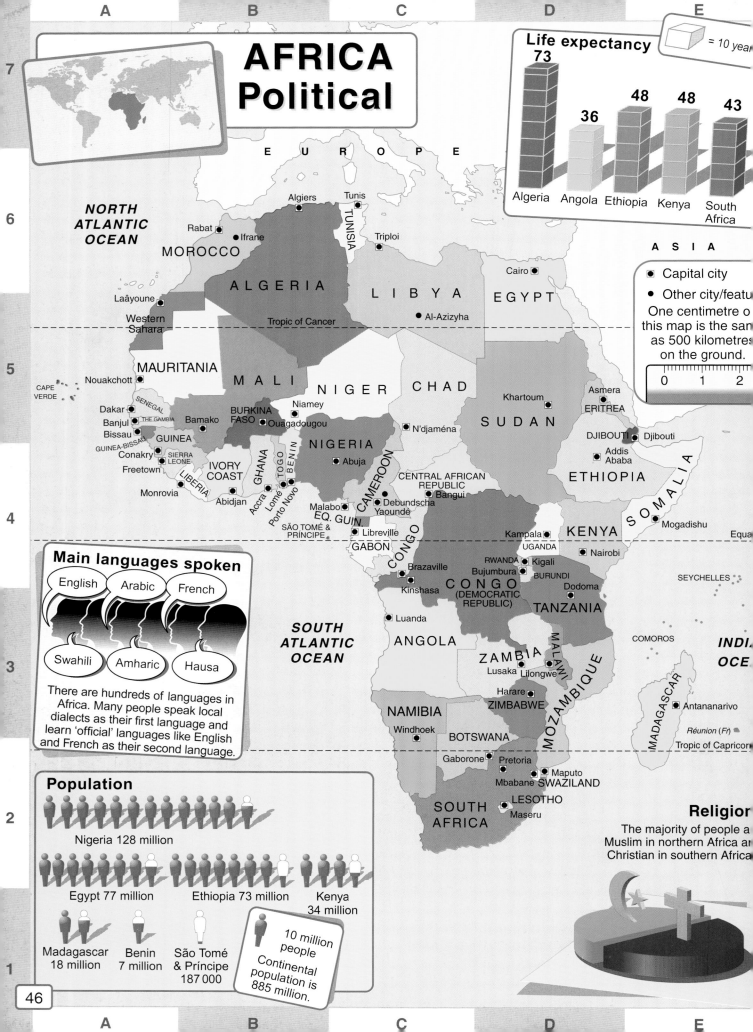

AFRICA
Political

Life expectancy
73
36
48
48
43
= 10 years
Algeria Angola Ethiopia Kenya South Africa

- Capital city
- Other city/feature

One centimetre o
this map is the sam
as 500 kilometre
on the ground.

0   1   2

EUROPE
ASIA

NORTH ATLANTIC OCEAN

SOUTH ATLANTIC OCEAN

INDI
OCE

Main languages spoken

English Arabic French
Swahili Amharic Hausa

There are hundreds of languages in Africa. Many people speak local dialects as their first language and learn 'official' languages like English and French as their second language.

Population

Nigeria 128 million

Egypt 77 million   Ethiopia 73 million   Kenya 34 million

Madagascar 18 million   Benin 7 million   São Tomé & Príncipe 187 000

10 million people
Continental population is 885 million.

Religion
The majority of people a
Muslim in northern Africa ar
Christian in southern Africa

Tropic of Cancer
Tropic of Capricor
Equa

Algiers Tunis TUNISIA
Rabat Ifrane Triploi
MOROCCO
ALGERIA LIBYA EGYPT Cairo
Al-Azizyha
Laâyoune
Western Sahara
MAURITANIA
Nouakchott MALI NIGER CHAD SUDAN Khartoum Asmera ERITREA
CAPE VERDE
Dakar SENEGAL BURKINA FASO Niamey N'djaména DJIBOUTI Djibouti
Banjul THE GAMBIA Bamako Ouagadougou NIGERIA Addis Ababa
Bissau GUINEA Abuja CAMEROON CENTRAL AFRICAN REPUBLIC ETHIOPIA SOMALIA
GUINEA-BISSAU Conakry SIERRA LEONE IVORY COAST GHANA TOGO BENIN Bangui Mogadishu
Freetown LIBERIA Malabo Debundscha Yaoundé
Monrovia Abidjan Accra Lomé Porto Novo EQ. GUIN. Libreville KENYA
SÃO TOMÉ & PRÍNCIPE GABON CONGO Kampala UGANDA Nairobi
Brazaville RWANDA Kigali
Kinshasa Bujumbura BURUNDI SEYCHELLES
CONGO (DEMOCRATIC REPUBLIC) Dodoma
Luanda TANZANIA
ANGOLA COMOROS
ZAMBIA MALAWI
Lusaka Lilongwe MOZAMBIQUE MADAGASCAR Antananarivo
Harare Réunion (Fr)
NAMIBIA ZIMBABWE
Windhoek BOTSWANA
Gaborone Pretoria Maputo
Mbabane SWAZILAND
SOUTH AFRICA LESOTHO Maseru

46

AFRICA Physical

▲	Mountains
	Highlands
▬	Lowlands
	Deserts

...y a few people live in ...Sahara Desert. ...se who do, travel ...ss it with their ...als on routes ...h have been ...d for ...turies.

...frica does not have the ...xtremes of temperature ...und in Asia and Europe. ...t is the warmest of the ...world's continents. The ...nly permanent snow is ...on mountains such as Kilimanjaro.

Canary Is.

Atlas Mts

▲ Mt Toubkal

Mediterranean Sea

S A H A R A

Tropic of Cancer

Fouta Djalon

Niger

Niger

Nile

Tibesti Massif

Nubian Desert

Red Sea

NORTH ATLANTIC OCEAN

Lake Volta

Lake Chad

Benue

Nile

Ethiopian Highlands

Gulf of Guinea

▲ Mt Cameroon

Zaire Basin

Ruwenzori Range

Lake Turkana

Zaire

Great Rift Valley

▲ Mt Kenya

Equator

Tanganyika

Lake

Lake Victoria

▲ Mt Kilimanjaro

INDIAN OCEAN

Zanzibar

Comoros

Lake Malawi

pic of Capricorn

SOUTH ATLANTIC OCEAN

Namib Desert

Zambezi

Lake Kariba

Kalahari Desert

Limpopo

Orange

Cape of Good Hope

Drakensberg

actfile

oldest place	Ilfrane (Morocco) −24°C
ottest place	Al-Aziziyha (Libya) 58°C
ettest place	Debundscha (Cameroon) 1 029 cm per year
ighest mountain	Mt Kilimanjaro (Tanzania) 5 895 m
ongest coastline	Madagascar 4 828 km
ongest river	Nile (Eygpt/Sudan) 6 670 km
argest lake	Lake Victoria (Uganda/Kenya/Tanzania) 69 400 km²

teresting facts:
he Sahara is the world's largest desert, stretching over 5 000 km
om east to west and over 2 000 km from north to south. It covers a
rger area than the whole of Australia.

The Great Rift Valley runs through East Africa.
It is nearly 9 000 km long. The great lakes of
East Africa are found in this enormous valley.

47

AFRICA Global Issues

Around the world, wildlife is und[er] threat. Some species have alrea[dy] disappeared forever. Others are [in] danger no[w]

The world elephant population

Elephants in Africa

- In the past
- Today

Tropic of Cancer

Equator

In Africa, the elephant population has been shrinking rapidly. There are three main reasons:
1. More and more of the land is used by people for farming. The elephants' habitat is therefore being destroyed.
2. Elephants have been killed for their ivory which can be sold for large amounts of money.
3. Changes in the climate.

Some countries have protected the elephants by providing nature reserves, where elephant numbers are controlled but elephants can enjoy a natural existence. The nature reserves attract tourists who bring much needed money to the area.

Tropic of Capricorn

Goods carved from ivory were once sold all around the world. Now most countries have agreed to ban the trade in ivory. When ivory is taken from poachers it is burned. This is to prevent the trade continuing.

What should anyone who cares about the future of elephants do if offered the chance to buy ivory products?

30 years ago	3 000 000 elephants
20 years ago	1 300 000
Today	600 000
?	The last elephant?

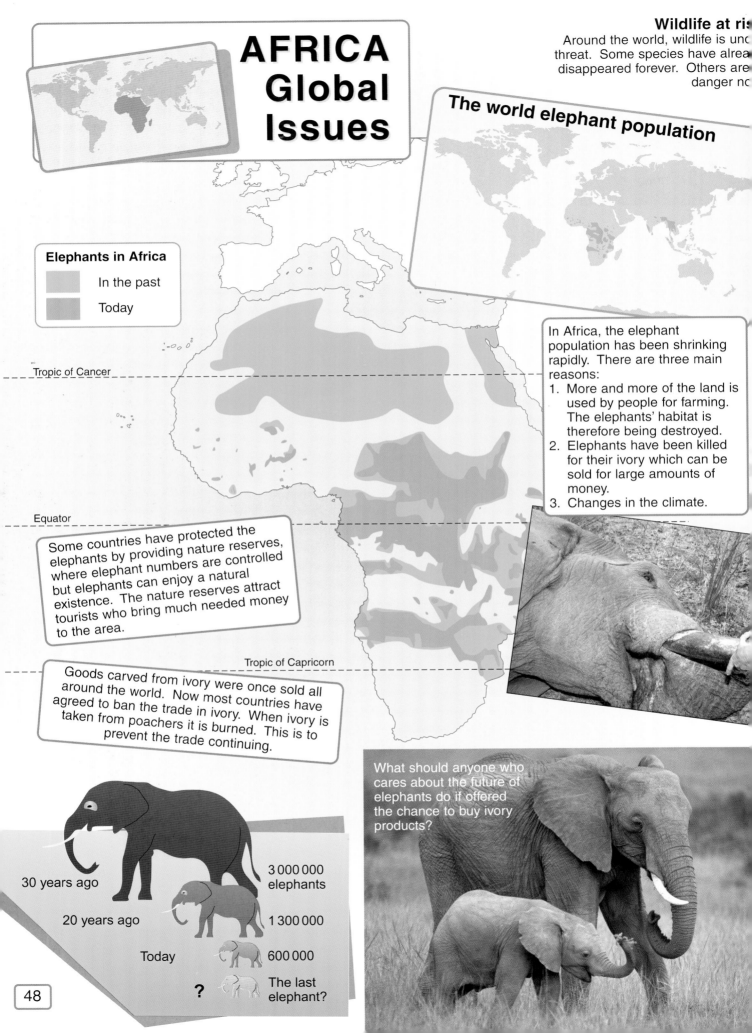

48

Deserts of the world

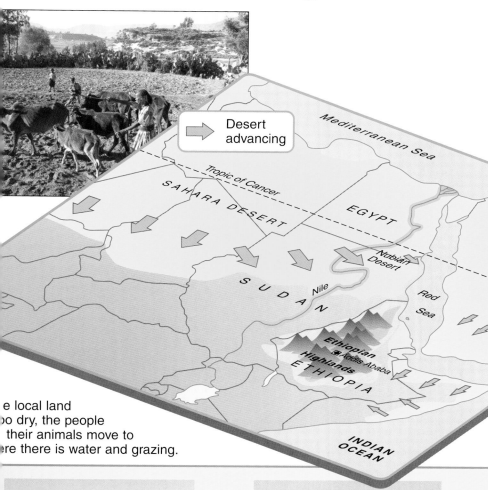

The area of the world covered by desert is increasing.

Advancing deserts

The rains which used to come regularly to Ethiopia and Sudan are no longer reliable. Without the rain, crops do not grow and the natural vegetation on which animals live is also damaged.

Desert advancing

Mediterranean Sea

Tropic of Cancer

SAHARA DESERT

EGYPT

SUDAN

Nubian Desert

Nile

Red Sea

Ethiopian Highlands
● Addis Ababa
ETHIOPIA

INDIAN OCEAN

As the population grows, more use is made of the land. More trees are chopped down for fuel, more animals graze and more forest is cleared for farming.

e local land
o dry, the people
their animals move to
re there is water and grazing.

The extra animals eat the young trees before they can grow.

Without the trees the soil becomes loose.

The loose soil is blown away, fewer crops grow and the land turns to desert.

49

SOUTH AMERICA Political

Life expectancy

= 10 years

Bolivia	Brazil	Ecuador	Peru	Uruguay
65	72	76	70	76

Religion

The most common religion in South America is Christianity.

Main languages spoken

Spanish   Quecha   Portugese

- ■ Capital city
- • Other city/feature

One centimetre on this map is the same as 500 kilometres on the ground.

0   1   2

Population

Brazil 186 million

Argentina 40 m   Peru 28 m   Chile 16 m

Bolivia 9 m   Uruguay 3.5 m   Surinam 0.5 m

10 million people
Continental population is 365 million.

CENTRAL AMERICA

PANAMA

Galápagos Is (Ecuador)

Caracas

VENEZUELA

Quibdó   ■ Bogotá

COLOMBIA

Georgetown
Paramaribo
Cayenne

GUYANA   SURINAME   French Guiana

Quito

ECUADOR

Equator

PERU

Lima

BRAZIL

NORTH ATLANTIC OCEAN

La Paz

BOLIVIA

Brasilia

PARAGUAY

Rio de Janeiro

São Paulo

Tropic of Capricorn

SOUTH ATLANTIC OCEAN

Rivadavia   Asunción

C H I L E

Santiago

ARGENTINA

Buenos Aires   URUGUAY   Montevideo

PACIFIC OCEAN

Sarmiento

Falkland Is. (UK)

Punta Arenas

Argentina attracted immigrants from many parts of Europe

Peru was once a part of the great Inca Empire. Markets like these have been held on the same sites since Inca times.

50

Amazonia

SOUTH AMERICA
Physical

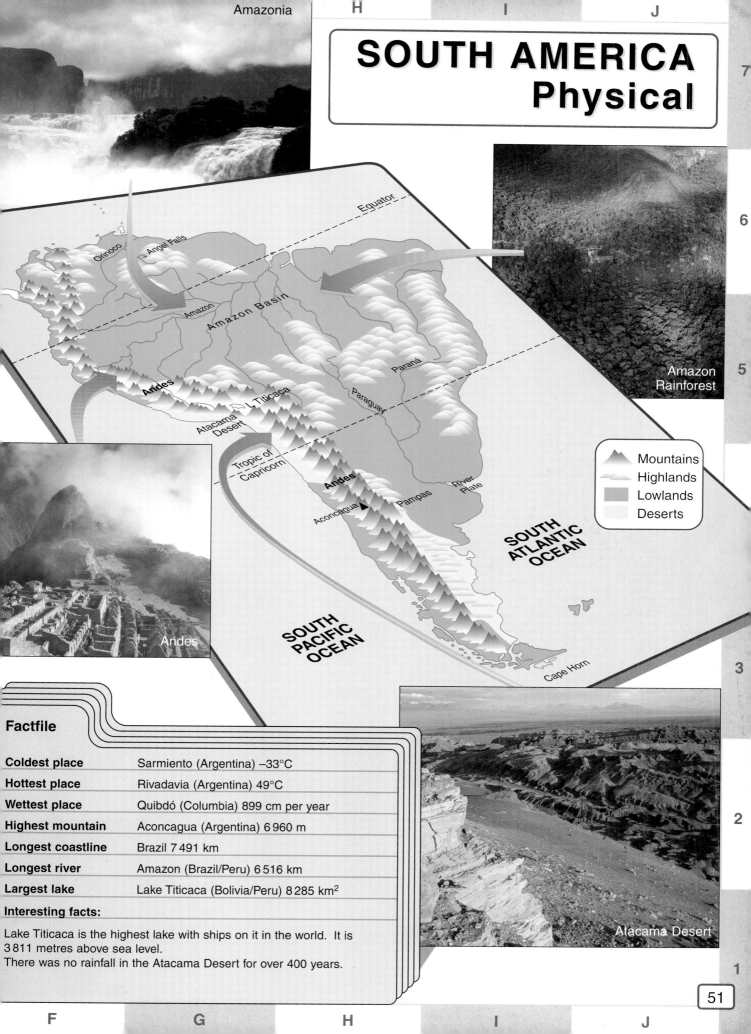

Equator

Orinoco

Angel Falls

Amazon

Amazon Basin

Paraná

Andes

L. Titicaca

Paraguay

Atacama
Desert

Tropic of
Capricorn

Andes

Aconcagua ▲

Pampas

River
Plate

6

5

Amazon
Rainforest

Andes

SOUTH
PACIFIC
OCEAN

SOUTH
ATLANTIC
OCEAN

Cape Horn

	Mountains
	Highlands
	Lowlands
	Deserts

3

Factfile

Coldest place	Sarmiento (Argentina) −33°C
Hottest place	Rivadavia (Argentina) 49°C
Wettest place	Quibdó (Columbia) 899 cm per year
Highest mountain	Aconcagua (Argentina) 6 960 m
Longest coastline	Brazil 7 491 km
Longest river	Amazon (Brazil/Peru) 6 516 km
Largest lake	Lake Titicaca (Bolivia/Peru) 8 285 km^2

Interesting facts:

Lake Titicaca is the highest lake with ships on it in the world. It is
3 811 metres above sea level.
There was no rainfall in the Atacama Desert for over 400 years.

Atacama Desert

2

1

51

F   G   H   I   J

SOUTH AMERICA
Global Issues

Tropical rainforests of the world

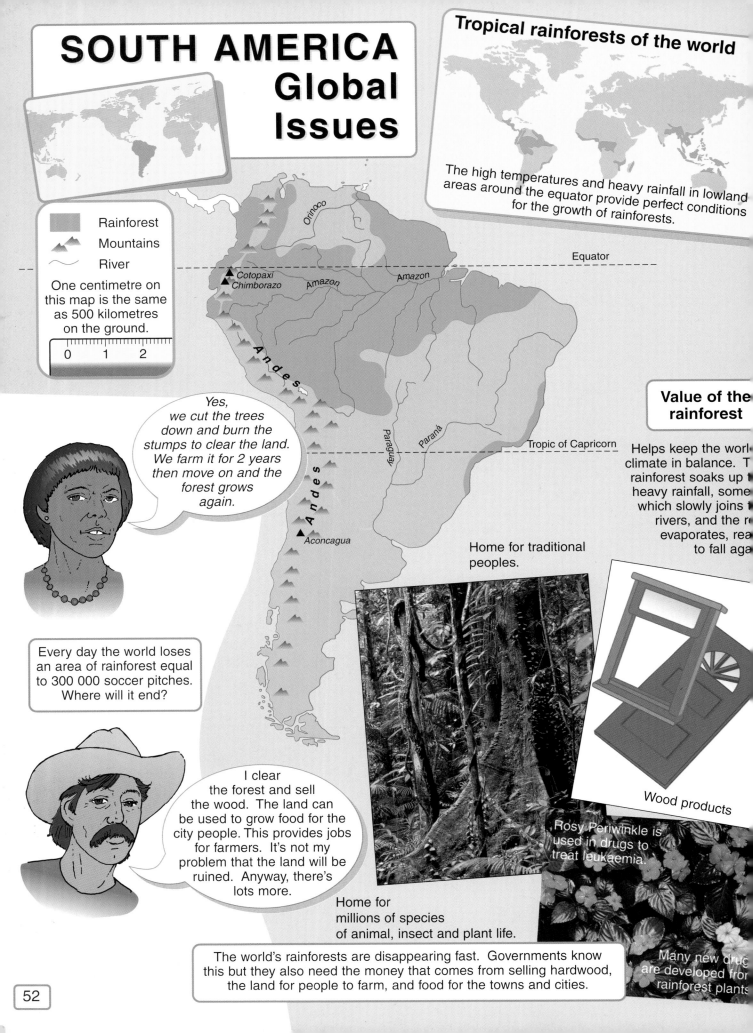

The high temperatures and heavy rainfall in lowland areas around the equator provide perfect conditions for the growth of rainforests.

Legend:
- Rainforest
- Mountains
- River

One centimetre on this map is the same as 500 kilometres on the ground.

0 1 2

Orinoco

Equator

Cotopaxi
Chimborazo

Amazon

Amazon

Andes

Paraguay

Paraná

Tropic of Capricorn

Andes

Aconcagua

Yes, we cut the trees down and burn the stumps to clear the land. We farm it for 2 years then move on and the forest grows again.

Every day the world loses an area of rainforest equal to 300 000 soccer pitches. Where will it end?

I clear the forest and sell the wood. The land can be used to grow food for the city people. This provides jobs for farmers. It's not my problem that the land will be ruined. Anyway, there's lots more.

Value of the rainforest

Helps keep the worl climate in balance. T rainforest soaks up heavy rainfall, some which slowly joins rivers, and the r evaporates, rea to fall aga

Home for traditional peoples.

Wood products

Rosy Periwinkle is used in drugs to treat leukaemia.

Home for millions of species of animal, insect and plant life.

The world's rainforests are disappearing fast. Governments know this but they also need the money that comes from selling hardwood, the land for people to farm, and food for the towns and cities.

Many new drug are developed fror rainforest plants

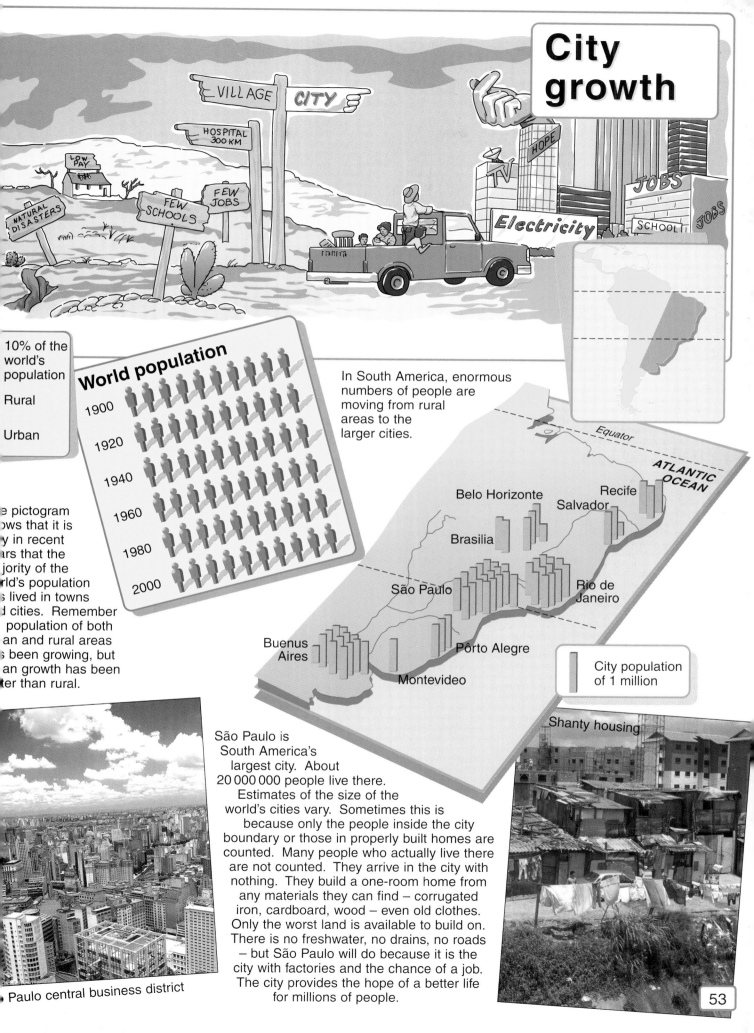

City growth

VILLAGE   CITY

HOSPITAL 300 KM

LOW PAY

NATURAL DISASTERS

FEW SCHOOLS   FEW JOBS

HOPE

TV

Electricity

JOBS

SCHOOL   JOBS

10% of the world's population

Rural

Urban

World population

1900

1920

1940

1960

1980

2000

e pictogram
ows that it is
y in recent
ars that the
jority of the
rld's population
s lived in towns
d cities. Remember
population of both
an and rural areas
s been growing, but
an growth has been
ter than rural.

In South America, enormous
numbers of people are
moving from rural
areas to the
larger cities.

Equator

ATLANTIC OCEAN

Belo Horizonte

Recife

Salvador

Brasilia

São Paulo

Rio de Janeiro

Buenus Aires

Pôrto Alegre

Montevideo

City population
of 1 million

Shanty housing

São Paulo is
South America's
largest city. About
20 000 000 people live there.
Estimates of the size of the
world's cities vary. Sometimes this is
because only the people inside the city
boundary or those in properly built homes are
counted. Many people who actually live there
are not counted. They arrive in the city with
nothing. They build a one-room home from
any materials they can find – corrugated
iron, cardboard, wood – even old clothes.
Only the worst land is available to build on.
There is no freshwater, no drains, no roads
– but São Paulo will do because it is the
city with factories and the chance of a job.
The city provides the hope of a better life
for millions of people.

Paulo central business district

53

NORTH AMERICA
Political

Life expectancy
$= 10$ years

67 Belize
77 Cuba
53 Haiti
75 Mexico
77 USA

Religion
The most common religion in North America is Christianity.

- ◉ Capital city
- ● Other city/feature

One centimetre on this map is the same as 500 kilometres on the ground.

0 1 2

The life of the native people in the far north of America has changed greatly in recent years.

Main languages spoken

English   Spanish

French

ARCTIC OCEAN

GREENLAND (Kalaallit Nunaat)
● Eismitte
◉ Nuuk (Godhaab)

Arctic Circle

C A N A D A

● Henderson Lake

Ottawa ◉

NORTH ATLANTIC OCEAN

DR. DOMINICAN REPUBLIC
ES. EL SALVADOR

NORTH PACIFIC OCEAN

Death Valley ●

U N I T E D   S T A T E S   O F   A M E R I C A

● Washington

Bermuda (UK)

Tropic of Cancer

THE BAHAMAS
◉ Nassau

M E X I C O

Havana ◉
CUBA

Puerto Rico *(USA)*

ST KITTS & N
ANTIGUA &
Guadelou
DOMINIC
Martini
ST LUCIA
ST VINCENT
GRENADA

Port Prince
HAITI

DR.

Santo Domingo

JAMAICA ◉ ◉ Kingston

Curacao (Neth)

TRINI
& TOB

◉ Mexico City

BELIZE
◉ Belmopan
HONDURAS
● Tegucigalpa
Guatemala City ◉
GUATEMALA ◉ ES. NICARAGUA
San Salvador ◉ Managua
COSTA RICA Panama
San José PANAMA City

Population

👤 10 million people
Continental population is 495 million.

USA 295 million

Mexico 106 million

Canada 33 million

Honduras 7 million
Nicaragua 5.5 million
Jamaica 2.75 million
Greenland 56 000

The USA is known as a 'mosaic'. People from all over the world have moved to the USA.

NORTH AMERICA
Physical

The climate in North America ranges from the freezing cold of the Arctic to the sub-tropical heat of Central America.

Coniferous forests, Canada

The Grand Canyon, Colorado River

ARCTIC OCEAN

NORTH PACIFIC OCEAN

Mt McKinley
Yukon
Mackenzie
Great Bear Lake
Arctic Circle
Great Slave Lake
Hudson Bay
Rocky Mountains
Missouri
Lake Winnepeg
L. Superior
Great Lakes
St Lawrence
Newfoundland
Oodaq
Greenland (Kalaallit Nunaat)
California
Great Salt Lake
Death Valley
Colorado
Great Plains
Mississippi
Appalachain Mts
Rio Grande
Sierra Madre
Gulf of Mexico
NORTH ATLANTIC OCEAN
Tropic of Cancer
Caribbean Sea
L. Nicaragua

Mountains
Highlands
Lowlands
Deserts
Ice cap

Factfile

Coldest place	Eismitte (Greenland) –64.8°C
Hottest place	Death Valley (USA) 57°C
Wettest place	Henderson Lake (Canada) 650 cm per year
Highest mountain	Mt McKinley (USA) 6 194 m
Longest coastline	Canada 90 908 km
Longest river	Mississippi/Missouri (USA) 6 019 km
Largest lake	Lake Superior (USA/Canada) 83 270 km²

Interesting facts:

The longest border in the world separates the USA and Canada. It is 6 416 km long. The world's largest trees are the Giant Sequoia in California. The nearest island to the North Pole is Oodaq, Greenland which is 706.4 km away.

The Bahamas

NORTH AMERICA
Global Issues

Water for life
Clean water is vitally important if people are to stay healthy. Diseases carried in water kill millions of people around the world every year.

Farmers require large quantities of water in order to grow crops such as grapes and cotton. Water is often taken from rivers.

Cities like Las Vegas have been built in dry parts of North America. Water for such cities has to be brought hundreds of kilometres.

The danger is that as cities grow the demand for water will increase and may be impossible to provide for the needs of the people. How can the use of water be reduced?

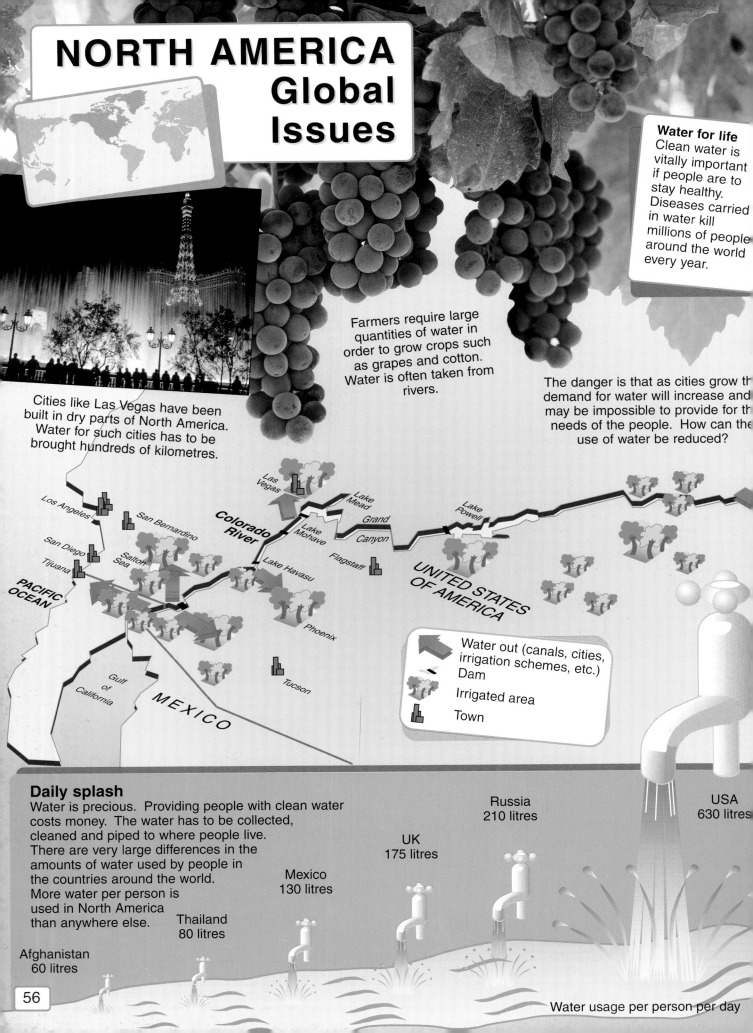

Las Vegas

Lake Mead

Grand

Lake Powell

Los Angeles

San Bernardino

Colorado River

Lake Mohave

Canyon

San Diego

Salton Sea

Tijuana

Lake Havasu

Flagstaff

UNITED STATES OF AMERICA

PACIFIC OCEAN

Phoenix

Tucson

Gulf of California

MEXICO

Water out (canals, cities, irrigation schemes, etc.)
Dam
Irrigated area
Town

Daily splash
Water is precious. Providing people with clean water costs money. The water has to be collected, cleaned and piped to where people live. There are very large differences in the amounts of water used by people in the countries around the world. More water per person is used in North America than anywhere else.

Russia 210 litres

USA 630 litres

UK 175 litres

Mexico 130 litres

Thailand 80 litres

Afghanistan 60 litres

Water usage per person per day

Tourism

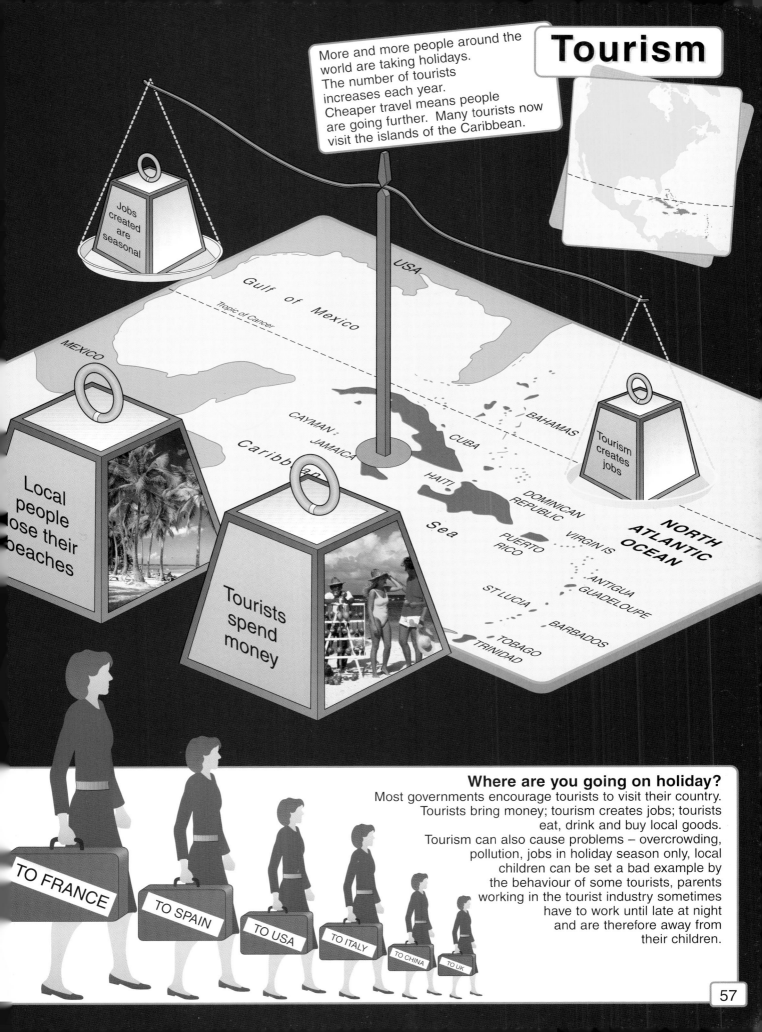

More and more people around the world are taking holidays. The number of tourists increases each year. Cheaper travel means people are going further. Many tourists now visit the islands of the Caribbean.

Jobs created are seasonal

Tourism creates jobs

Local people lose their beaches

Tourists spend money

Gulf of Mexico

Tropic of Cancer

USA

MEXICO

CAYMAN

JAMAICA

Caribbean

Sea

HAITI

CUBA

BAHAMAS

DOMINICAN REPUBLIC

PUERTO RICO

VIRGIN IS

ST LUCIA

ANTIGUA

GUADELOUPE

BARBADOS

TOBAGO

TRINIDAD

NORTH ATLANTIC OCEAN

TO FRANCE

TO SPAIN

TO USA

TO ITALY

TO CHINA

TO UK

Where are you going on holiday?
Most governments encourage tourists to visit their country. Tourists bring money; tourism creates jobs; tourists eat, drink and buy local goods.
Tourism can also cause problems – overcrowding, pollution, jobs in holiday season only, local children can be set a bad example by the behaviour of some tourists, parents working in the tourist industry sometimes have to work until late at night and are therefore away from their children.

AUSTRALASIA
Political

Life expectancy

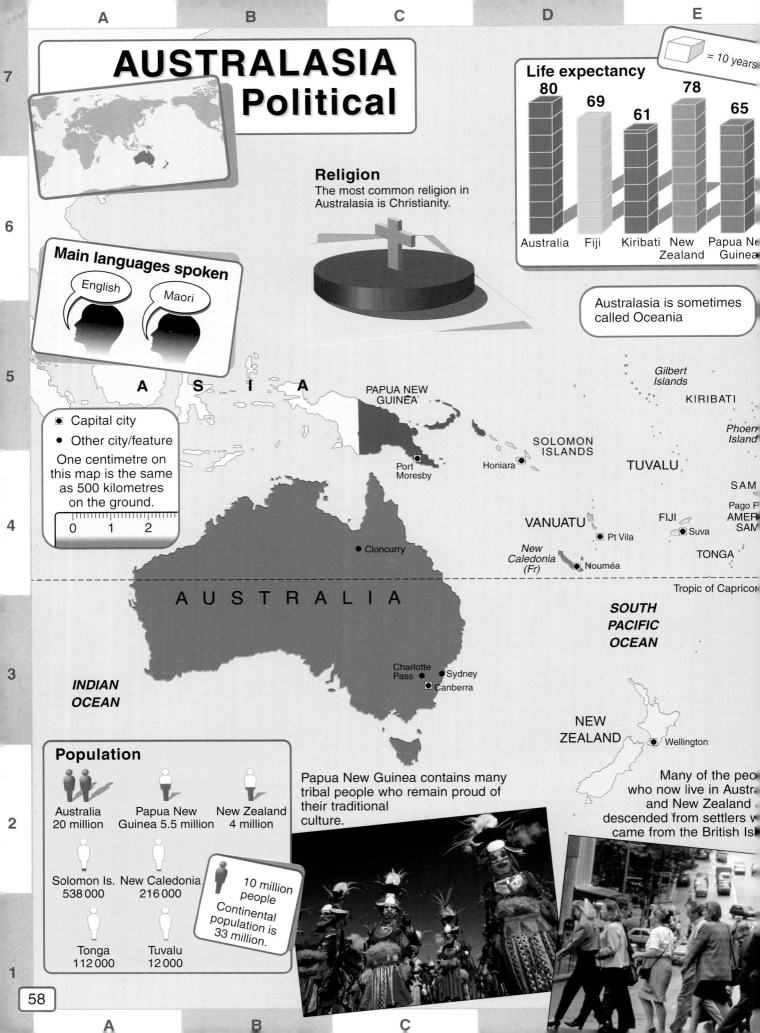

= 10 years

80 Australia
69 Fiji
61 Kiribati
78 New Zealand
65 Papua New Guinea

Religion
The most common religion in Australasia is Christianity.

Australasia is sometimes called Oceania

Main languages spoken
English
Maori

- ▣ Capital city
- ● Other city/feature

One centimetre on this map is the same as 500 kilometres on the ground.

0   1   2

A S I A

PAPUA NEW GUINEA

Gilbert Islands

KIRIBATI

SOLOMON ISLANDS

Phoenix Islands

Port Moresby

Honiara

TUVALU

SAM

VANUATU

Pago P

FIJI

AMER

● Cloncurry

New Caledonia (Fr)

▣ Pt Vila

▣ Suva

SAM

A U S T R A L I A

▣ Nouméa

TONGA

Tropic of Capricor

SOUTH PACIFIC OCEAN

INDIAN OCEAN

Charlotte Pass ●
● Sydney
▣ Canberra

NEW ZEALAND
● Wellington

Population

Australia 20 million

Papua New Guinea 5.5 million

New Zealand 4 million

Solomon Is. 538 000

New Caledonia 216 000

10 million people
Continental population is 33 million.

Tonga 112 000

Tuvalu 12 000

Papua New Guinea contains many tribal people who remain proud of their traditional culture.

Many of the peo
who now live in Austra
and New Zealand
descended from settlers
came from the British Is

AUSTRALASIA
Physical

rs Rock (Uluru) is a great
ist attraction. The Aborigines
ard it as a sacred site.

The climate varies
from the equatorial
heat and heavy rain
of Papua New
Guinea to the mild
climate of South
Island, New Zealand
with its snow-capped
mountains.

Rainforest, Papua
New Guinea

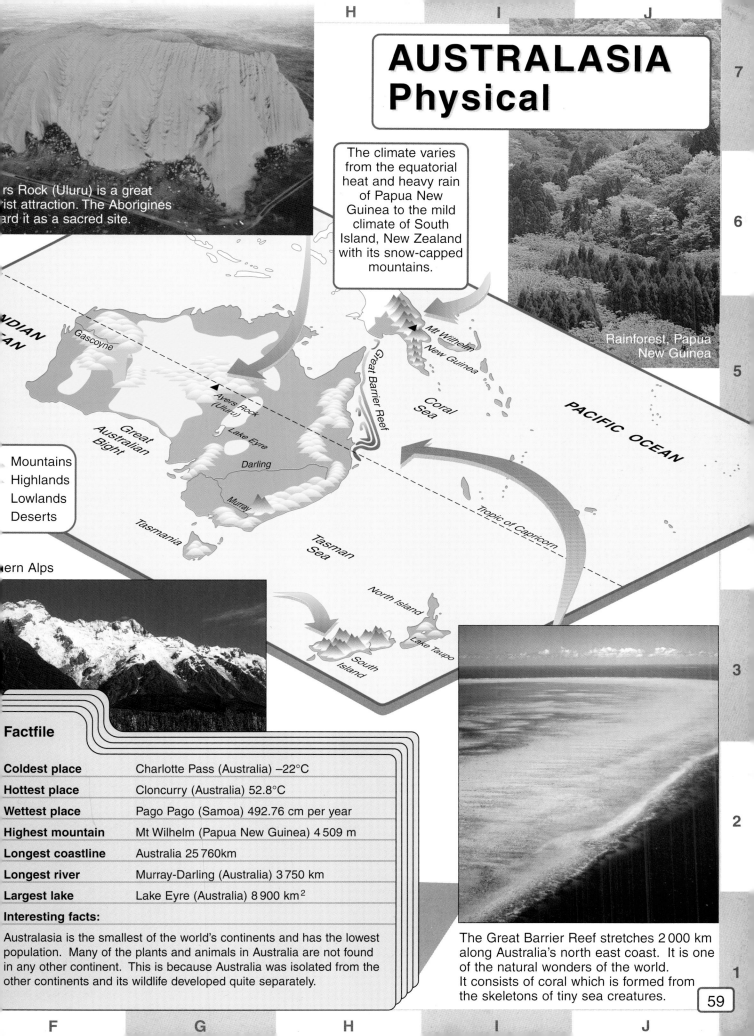

NDIAN
CAN

Gascoyne

Mt Wilhelm
New Guinea

Great Barrier Reef

Coral
Sea

PACIFIC OCEAN

Ayers Rock
(Uluru)

Lake Eyre

Great
Australian
Bight

Darling

Mountains
Highlands
Lowlands
Deserts

Murray

Tropic of Capricorn

Tasmania

Tasman
Sea

North Island

Lake Taupo

ern Alps

South
Island

Factfile

Coldest place	Charlotte Pass (Australia) −22°C
Hottest place	Cloncurry (Australia) 52.8°C
Wettest place	Pago Pago (Samoa) 492.76 cm per year
Highest mountain	Mt Wilhelm (Papua New Guinea) 4 509 m
Longest coastline	Australia 25 760km
Longest river	Murray-Darling (Australia) 3 750 km
Largest lake	Lake Eyre (Australia) 8 900 km^2

Interesting facts:

Australasia is the smallest of the world's continents and has the lowest
population. Many of the plants and animals in Australia are not found
in any other continent. This is because Australia was isolated from the
other continents and its wildlife developed quite separately.

The Great Barrier Reef stretches 2 000 km
along Australia's north east coast. It is one
of the natural wonders of the world.
It consists of coral which is formed from
the skeletons of tiny sea creatures.

ANTARCTICA

This picture shows Antarctica viewed from the south. Compare this with Antarctica shown flat on the world map

Who claims Antarctica?

A number of countries claim parts of Antarctica, however in October 1991 it was agreed that no attempts would be made to discover or remove the rich minerals which lie under the ground of Antarctica. This is to last until the year 2041.

Population

Apart from scientists, no people live in Antarctica, however it is home for many land and sea animals as well as birds.

ATLANTIC OCEAN

Antarctic Circle

INDIAN OCEAN

Antarctic Peninsula

Ronne Ice Shelf

ANTARCTICA

Vinson Massif ▲

Transatlantic Mountains

✕ South Pole

• Vostok

Ross Ice shelf

Antarctic Circle

PACIFIC OCEAN

Ice shelf

Mountain

One centimetre on this map is the same as 500 kilometres on the ground.

0   1   2

A hole in the ozo[ne]

Above the Earth is the *ozo[ne] layer,* which absorbs dangerou[s] rays from the sun. Pollutio[n] causing holes to appear in t[he] layer over the Antarctic. Th[ere] is the danger that this will affect [the] ocean and will kill the k[rill] (small shrimp-like creature[s]. Without k[rill] wha[les] seals a[nd] sea bi[rds] will surv[ive]

Sun's rays

layer

ozone

ice

Factfile

Coldest place	Vostok −89°C
Highest mountain	Vinson Massif 5 140 m
Human population	A few scientists

Interesting facts:

Antarctica contains 90% of the world's ice.
The first person to reach the South Pole was Roald Amundsen in 1911.
There is continuous daylight from November to February.
It is as dry as the Sahara desert.

Much of the Antarctic is covered in a sheet of ice, some of it thousands of metres thick. If the Earth's temperature rises and the ice begins to melt then sea levels will rise causing floodi[ng]

THE ARCTIC CIRCLE

imals of the Arctic

y animals live within the Arctic Circle on the
, on the ice and in the sea.

> The Arctic does not consist of land. What we see on the map is not a continent but frozen ice. Submarines can sail under this ice.

Arctic Circle

ARCTIC OCEAN

North
+
Pole

any air routes
ss the Arctic.
ou use a globe
u will see that
shortest route
tween many
es is across
the Arctic.

Extent of frozen ice
— Air route

Tokyo

Beijing

Anchorage • USA

Vancouver •

C A N A D A

R U S S I A

GREENLAND
(Kalaallit Nunaat)

Mt Gunnbjorn ▲

Chicago •

Toronto •

New York •

ICELAND

NORWAY
SWEDEN
FINLAND

Moscow •
Helsinki •
Stockholm •

Oslo •

Warsaw •

Berlin •

Ankara •

London •

Paris •

Rome •

Madrid •

> Land in North America, northern Europe and Asia is inside the Arctic Circle. A variety of different peoples live there. The Inuit live there all year round. The Sami (Lapps) take their reindeer there during the summer months.

ctfile

ghest mountain	Gunnbjorn 3 700 m
man population	Inuit live in the Arctic all year.
	Sami live there in the summer.

eresting facts:

ring the summer the sun shines throughout the day
d night, but the temperature rarely rises above 10°C.

INTERNATIONAL TIME ZONES

Wherever we live in the world, when the sun rises in the east we call it morning. When it is the middle of the day Hong Kong it is the middle of the night in New York.

We divide the world map up into 24 zones, the same as the 24 hours in the day.

When the countries of the world agreed to a common world map showing lines longitude the start line was drawn through Greenwich in England. At that time sail used the world map more than anyone else and the British navy was the world's largest.

The time zones sometimes bend because some countries find it convenient to keep the same time across the whole country. Other countries like the USA, Canada, Australia and Russia have a number of time zones.

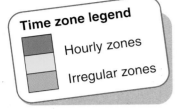

Time zone legend

Hourly zones

Irregular zones

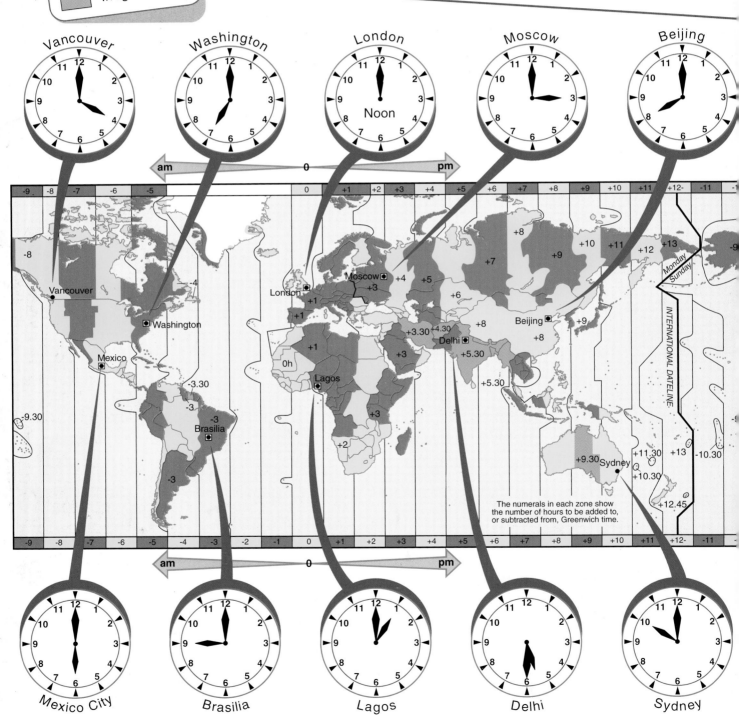

The numerals in each zone show the number of hours to be added to, or subtracted from, Greenwich time.

Limpopo *River* Africa 47 C3
Line Islands North Pacific Ocean 35
Lisbon Portugal 38 E2
LITHUANIA Europe 38 D4
Ljubljana Slovenia 38 D3
Loire *River* France 39 B4
Lomé Togo 46 B4
London United Kingdom 38 D2
Luanda Angola 46 C3
Lusaka Zambia 46 D3
LUXEMBOURG Europe 38 D3

M
MACEDONIA Europe 38 E4
Mackenzie *River* Canada 55 H6
Macquarie *Island* South Pacific Ocean 35
MADAGASCAR Africa 46 E3
Madeira Islands North Atlantic Ocean 34
Madrid Spain 38 E2
Malabo Equatorial Guinea 46 C4
MALAWI Africa 46 D3
MALAYSIA Asia 42 E4
MALDIVES Indian Ocean 35
MALI Africa 46 B5
Malin Sea Europe 39 B5
MALTA *Island* Europe 38 E3
Managua Nicaragua 54 D2
Manila Phillipines 42 E4
Maputo Mozambique 46 D2
Marcus Island North Pacific Ocean 35
Mariana Islands North Pacific Ocean 35
Marquesas Islands South Pacific Ocean 35
Marshall Islands North Pacific Ocean 35
Martinique Island Central America 54 E2
Maseru Lesotho 46 D2
MAURITANIA Africa 46 A5
MAURITIUS Indian Ocean 46 E3
Mbabane Swaziland 46 D2
Mediterranean Sea Europe/Asia 39 D3
Mekong *River* Asia 43 B4
MEXICO Central America 54 C2
Mexico City Mexico 54 C2
Midway Islands North Pacific Ocean 35
Minsk Belarus 38 D4
Mississippi *River* USA 55 H4
Missouri *River* USA 55 H4
Mogadishu Somalia 46 E4
MOLDOVA Europe 38 D4
MONGOLIA Asia 42 C3
Monrovia Liberia 46 B4
MONTENEGRO Europe 38 E4
Montevideo Uruguay 50 C3
MOROCCO Africa 46 B6
Moscow Russia 38 D5
Mount Cameroon Cameroon 47 C5
Mount Elbrus Russia 39 E4
Mount Everest Asia 43 B4
Mount Gunnbjorn Greenland 61 H3
Mount Kenya Kenya 47 D4
Mount Kilimanjaro Tanzania 47 D4
Mount McKinley USA 55 H6
Mount Toubkal Morocco 47 C6
Mount Wilhelm Papua New Guinea 59 H5
MOZAMBIQUE Africa 46 D3
Murray *River* Australia 59 G4
Muscat Oman 42 E2
MYANMAR Asia 42 D3

N
Nairobi Kenya 46 D4
Namib Desert Namibia 47 B3
NAMIBIA Africa 46 C3
Nassau Bahamas 54 D3
N'djaména Chad 46 C5
NEPAL Asia 42 D3
NETHERLANDS Europe 38 D3
New Caledonia *Islands* Australasia 58 D4
New Delhi India 42 D3
New Guinea *Island* Australasia 59 H5
NEW ZEALAND Australasia 58 D3

Newfoundland Canada 55 J4
Niamey Niger 46 B5
NICARAGUA Central America 54 D2
NIGER Africa 46 C5
Niger *River* Africa 47 B5
NIGERIA Africa 46 C5
Nile *River* Africa 47 D5
Niue *Island* South Pacific Ocean 35
NORTH AMERICA 54
North Atlantic Ocean 36
North Island New Zealand 59 H3
NORTH KOREA Asia 42 D4
North Pacific Ocean 37
North Pole Arctic Circle 61 H4
North Sea Europe 39 B4
NORWAY Europe 38 C3
Norwegian Sea Europe 39 B5
Nouakchott Mauritania 46 A5
Nouméa New Caledonia 58 D4
Nubian Desert Africa 47 E5
Nuuk Greenland 54 D5

O
Oceania *see* Australasia
Oman Asia 42 E2
Orange *River* South Africa 47 B3
Orinoco *River* Venezuela 47 F6
Oslo Norway 38 C3
Ottawa Canada 54 D4
Ouagadougou Burkina Faso 46 B5

P
Pacific Ocean 37
Pago Pago Samoa 58 E4
PAKISTAN Asia 42 D2
Pampas *Feature* Argentina 47 H4
PANAMA Central America 54 D2
Panama City Panama 54 D2
PAPUA NEW GUINEA Australasia 58 C5
Paraguay *River* Argentina 47 H5
PARAGUAY South America 50 C4
Paramaribo Surinam 50 D6
Parana *River* South America 47 H5
Paris France 38 D2
Persian Gulf Asia 43 A4
Philippine Sea Asia 43 C5
PHILLIPINES Asia 42 E4
Phnom Penh Cambodia 42 E4
Phoenix Islands Kiribati 58 E5
Po *River* Italy 39 C4
POLAND Europe 38 D4
Port au Prince Haiti 54 D2
Port Moresby Papua New Guinea 58 C4
Port Vila Vanuatu 58 D4
Porto Novo Benin 46 B4
PORTUGAL Europe 38 E2
Prague Czech Republic 38 D3
Pretoria South Africa 46 D2
Prince Edward Islands South Atlantic Ocean 34
Puerto Rico *Island* Central America 54 E2
Pyongyang North Korea 42 D4
Pyrennes *Mountains* France/Spain 39 C4

Q
Qatar Asia 42 D2
Quito Ecuador 50 B5

R
Rabat Morocco 46 B6
Rangoon *see* Yangon
Red Sea Africa/Asia 47 E5
REPUBLIC OF IRELAND Europe 38 D2
Réunion *Island* Indian Ocean 46 E3
Revilla Gigedo Islands North Pacific Ocean 34
Reykjavik Iceland 38 C1
Rhine *River* Europe 39 C4
Rhône *River* Europe 39 C4
Riga Latvia 38 C4
Rio de Janeiro Brazil 50 D4
Rio Grande *River* North America 55 G4
River Plate South America 47 I4
Riyadh Saudi Arabia 42 D2

Rocky *Mountains* North America 55 H4
ROMANIA Europe 38 E4
Rome Italy 38 E3
Ronne Ice Shelf Antarctica 60 B5
Ross Ice Shelf Antarctica 60 C4
RUSSIA Asia 42 B3
RUSSIA Europe 38 C5
Ruwenzori Range *Mountains* Uganda/Zaire 47 D4
RWANDA Africa 46 D4

S
Sahara Desert Africa 47 C5
SAMOA Australasia 58 E4
San Ambrosio *Island* South Pacific Ocean 35
San José Costa Rica 54 D2
SAN MARINO Europe 38 E3
San Salvador El Salvador 54 D2
Sana Yemen 42 E2
Santiago Chile 50 C3
Santo Domingo Dominican Republic 54 E2
São Paulo Brazil 50 D4
SAO TOME & PRINCIPE Africa 46 C4
Sarajevo Bosnia Herzegovina 38 E4
Saudi Arabia Asia 42 D2
Scotia Sea South America 36
Sea of Japan Asia 43 D4
Sea of Okhotsk Russia 37
SENEGAL Africa 46 A5
Seoul South Korea 42 D4
SERBIA Europe 38 E4
SEYCHELLES Indian Ocean 46 E4
Shannon *River* Republic of Ireland 39 B4
Siberia *Feature* Russia 43 D5
SIERRA LEONE Africa 46 B4
Sierra Madre *Mountains* Mexico 55 G3
SINGAPORE Asia 42 E4
Singapore Singapore 42 E4
Skopje Macedonia 38 E4
SLOVAKIA Europe 38 D4
SLOVENIA Europe 38 D3
Socotra Indian Ocean 35
Sofia Bulgaria 38 E4
SOLOMON ISLANDS Australasia 58 D4
SOMALIA Africa 46 E4
SOUTH AFRICA Africa 46 C2
SOUTH AMERICA 50
South Atlantic Ocean 36
South China Sea Asia 43 C5
South Georgia *Island* South Atlantic Ocean 34
South Island New Zealand 59 H3
SOUTH KOREA Asia 42 D4
South Pacific Ocean 37
South Pole Antarctica 60 C4
South Sandwich Islands South Atlantic Ocean 34
SPAIN Europe 38 E2
SRI LANKA Asia 42 E3
St Helena Island South Atlantic Ocean 34
ST KITTS AND NEVIS Central America 54 E2
St Lawrence *River* USA 55 I4
ST LUCIA Central America 54 E2
St Paul Island Indian Ocean 35
ST VINCENT Central America 54 E2
Steppes *Feature* Asia 43 B5
Stockholm Sweden 38 C4
SUDAN Africa 46 D5
Sumatera *Island* Indonesia 43 B3
SURINAM South America 50 C6
Suva Fiji 58 E4
Svalbard Islands Arctic Ocean 34
SWAZILAND Africa 46 D2
SWEDEN Europe 38 C3
SWITZERLAND Europe 38 D3
Sydney Australia 58 C3
SYRIA Asia 42 D1

T
Tagus *River* Portugal 39 B3
Taipei Asia 42 D4
TAIWAN Asia 42 D4

TAJIKSTAN Asia 42 D2
Tallinn Estonia 38 C4
TANZANIA Africa 46 D3
Tashkent Uzbekistan 42 D2
Tasman Sea Australasia 59 H4
Tasmania Island Australia 59 G4
Tblisi Georgia 42 C2
Tegucigalpa Honduras 54 D2
Tehran Iran 42 D2
Tel Aviv Israel 42 D1
THAILAND Asia 42 E3
Thames *River* United Kingdom 39
Thimphu Bhutan 42 D3
Tibesti Massif *Mountains* Africa 4 D5
Tien Shan *Mountains* Asia 43 B5
Timor *Island* Indonesia 44
Tirana Albania 38 E4
TOGO Africa 46 B4
Tokelau Islands Pacific Ocean 35
Tokyo Japan 42 D5
TONGA Australasia 58 E4
Transantarctic *Mountains* Antarctic 60 C4
TRINIDAD AND TOBAGO Central America 54 E2
Tripoli Libya 46 C6
Tristan da Cunha *Island* South Atla Ocean 34
Tuamotu Archipelago *Islands* Sout Pacific Ocean 35
Tunis Tunisia 46 C6
TUNISIA Africa 46 C6
TURKEY Asia 42 D1
TURKEY Europe 38 E4
TURKMENISTAN Asia 42 D2
TUVALU Australasia 58 E4

U
UGANDA Africa 46 D4
UKRAINE Europe 38 D4
Ulan Bator Mongolia 42 C4
United Arab Emirates Asia 42 D2
UNITED KINGDOM Europe 38 D2
UNITED STATES OF AMERICA Nor America 54 C3
Ural *Mountains* Europe 39 E5
URUGUAY South America 50 C4
UZBEKISTAN Asia 42 D2

V
VANUATU Australasia 58 D4
VENEZUELA South America 50 C6
Vienna Austria 38 D3
Vientiane LAOS 42 D4
VIETNAM Asia 42 E4
Vinius Lithuania 38 D4
Vinson Masif *Mountain* Antarctica B4
Volga *River* Russia 39 D5
Vostok Antarctica 60 D4

W
Wake Island North Pacific Ocean
Warsaw Poland 38 D4
Washington USA 54 D3
Wellington New Zealand 58 E3
WESTERN SAHARA Africa 46 A5
WESTERN SAMOA 35
Windhoek Namibia 46 C3

Y
Yangon Myanmar 42 E3
Yangtze *River* China 43 C4
Yaoundé Cameroon 46 C4
Yellow Sea Asia 37
YEMEN Asia 42 E2
Yerevan Armenia 42 D2
Yukon *River* North America 55 H

Z
Zagreb Croatia 38 D3
Zaire Basin *Feature* Zaire 47 C4
Zaire *River* Zaire 47 B4
Zambezi *River* Africa 47 C3
ZAMBIA Africa 46 D3
Zanzibar Indian Ocean 47 D4
ZIMBABWE Africa 46 D3